MANUAL

# Basic TV Technology: Digital and Analog

**Fourth Edition**

**media**

MANUAL

Series editor: Peter Ward

# Basic TV Technology: Digital and Analog

## Fourth Edition

Robert L. Hartwig

ELSEVIER

AMSTERDAM • BOSTON • HEIDELBERG • LONDON • NEW YORK • OXFORD
PARIS • SAN DIEGO • SAN FRANCISCO • SINGAPORE • SYDNEY • TOKYO
Focal Press is an imprint of Elsevier

Focal Press

Focal Press is an imprint of Elsevier
30 Corporate Drive, Suite 400, Burlington, MA 01803, USA
Linacre House, Jordan Hill, Oxford OX2 8DP, UK

∞ Recognizing the importance of preserving what has been written, Elsevier prints
its books on acid-free paper whenever possible.

**Library of Congress Cataloging-in-Publication Data:**
Hartwig, Robert L.
  Basic TV technology : digital and analog / Robert L. Hartwig.—4th ed.
    p. cm.
  Includes bibliographical references and index.
  ISBN-13: 978-0-240-80717-1    ISBN-10: 0-240-80717-0
  1. Television–Handbooks, manuals, etc. I. Title.

TK6642.H37 2005
621.388—dc22

                                                                2005040004

**British Library Cataloguing-in-Publication Data**
A catalogue record for this book is available from the British Library.

**ISBN-13:** 978-0-240-80717-1
**ISBN-10:** 0-240-80717-0

For information on all Focal Press publications
visit our website at www.books.elsevier.com

05 06 07 08 09 10 11 10 9 8 7 6 5 4 3 2
Printed in the United States of America

Working together to grow
libraries in developing countries

www.elsevier.com | www.bookaid.org | www.sabre.org

ELSEVIER    BOOK AID International    Sabre Foundation

# Contents

**viii**

# Introduction

This is not a TV production textbook but a book for TV production people. It doesn't deal with TV production techniques because there are already several fine books that cover those subjects. I see no reason to write what others have already done a better job of writing. Rather, this book deals with two interrelated subjects. I will show you how the various pieces of video equipment are integrated to form a complex video system. But to understand that, you must first have some knowledge of how the equipment works and what goes on inside it. I will explain that as well.

As TV equipment becomes more complex and sophisticated, it becomes more important to understand how that equipment works. This is especially true in the worlds of instructional and industrial TV, where one person may have to do it all.

Having an understanding of how the equipment and systems work gives you two distinct advantages. First, you will be more adaptable to different makes, models, and features. New buttons and knobs aren't as likely to intimidate you. Second, you can be more creative. You're not limited to what you have been shown, but can figure out new applications and how to solve problems for yourself.

One need not be an engineer or know advanced math and physics to understand the basics of how TV equipment works. After teaching much of this material for more than 30 years, I know that students with little or no math and science background can be taught to understand the equipment. However, students must realize that, because of their lack of background, they may not be able to get detailed answers to all of their questions.

Based on feedback from former students and their employers, I'm confident that the material in this book is the single most important body of material that my TV students receive. Many of them feel that it's even more important than experience using the equipment.

Since this book deals with television systems, it's difficult to understand some topics without the proper foundation. This book, then, uses the building block approach. Many topics rely on information from previous topics. Most of this book should be studied sequentially.

I've attempted to make this book as easy to read and understand as possible, but it should be recognized that few of us can learn TV production or TV systems just from a book. The best learning will take place if you use this book in conjunction with hands-on TV production experience. Everything from directing to shading to tape operation will help make the contents of this book more meaningful. I've tried to make the text clear, concise, and conversational.

With digital technology having taken over the video world, some may wonder why there is so much analog material in this new edition. That is a fair question. All of the digital equipment we have today was based on the analog systems that came before. It is difficult to understand the new systems without some understanding of earlier analog technology. Some readers may feel that I have included too much information on analog, but I always feel it is better to know too much rather than not enough. That is why I have left so much analog in this edition.

Since my main goal is to help people understand the concepts, I have, on occasion, simplified the facts and various theories somewhat in order to make the concepts a little clearer. I hope more knowledgeable readers will not oppose these changes.

# Acknowledgments

The contents of this book have been accumulated over a period of years. Much of this technical information was generously supplied by patient engineers who were willing to take the time to share their field with one who was less knowledgeable.

Among them were the engineering staff at the TV studio of California State University, Chico, who, in my student days, were always willing to answer the technical questions that weren't covered in class. The man who designed and supervised the building and upgrade of our studio at Cuesta College, Darrell Wenhardt, of CBT Systems in San Diego, always found the time to discuss and explain emerging technologies, even years after his contractual obligations to the school had ended. Finally, I've been fortunate with regard to the maintenance engineers I've known at Cuesta College. Ken James, Jan Schaafsma, and currently Bill Bordeaux spent many hours of discussion helping me to expand my knowledge of this field.

I owe a special thanks to two people in particular. Professor Donald R. Mott of Butler University carefully read the first edition manuscript, and his detailed comments contributed greatly, making that edition a better book. I hope that this edition follows in the footsteps he helped direct. Darrell Wenhardt of CBT Systems has come through with many appreciated comments and suggestions for every edition of this book. Darrell keeps me on my toes, and his friendly prodding pushes me to stay current.

Five others have made strong contributions to this edition. Ian Bolt, University of Leeds; Brendan Casey, SUNY, Plattsburgh; Milton Chen, Stanford University; Michael Ogden, Central Washington University; and Christine White, Loughborough University, have reviewed various stages of the manuscript and have made many useful suggestions.

A special thanks goes to the people at Focal Press. When I started the first edition of this book, I had no idea how much editors, production people, and others added to the finished product; I thought it was the author who made the book. I know better now. The questioning, prodding, suggesting, refining, editing, and support by Christine Tridente and Elinor Actipis have made this a much better work than the one I originally created.

# The Atom and Electricity

In order to understand the technical aspects of television systems and equipment, it is important to know some basic theories, terms, and abbreviations in the field of electricity and electronics.

## The Parts of the Atom

The first thing to do is get a basic understanding of how electricity works. If you think back to your high school science classes, you'll recall that an atom is made up of three parts. The neutron is in the center or nucleus of the atom and has no electrical charge. Protons, also in the nucleus of the atom, have a positive charge ($+$). Like the planets circling the sun in the solar system, electrons circle the nucleus and have a negative charge ($-$). Since, for most elements, there are the same number of protons and electrons, the atom as a whole has no electrical charge.

## The Flow of Electrons through Metals

In some elements, usually the elements that we call metals, electrons can be very easily dislodged from their orbits. When they are knocked out of their orbits, they are attracted to other atoms and knock these atoms' electrons from their orbits. This flow of electrons is electricity. Of course, the atoms that have lost electrons now have an overall positive charge and tend to attract the loose electrons.

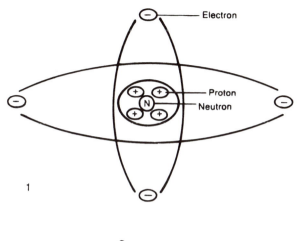

1

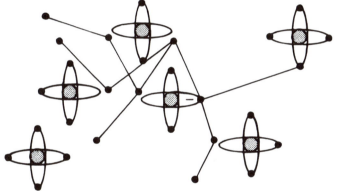

2

1. The parts of the atom.

2. The flow of electrons.

# Basic Circuits

### Direct Current (DC)

A flashlight battery has the ability to provide a flow of electrons but accomplishes nothing sitting on the shelf, since it is only stored energy. Only when the positive terminal of the battery is attached to one end of a light bulb and the other end of the light bulb is attached to the negative terminal of the battery do we have a completed circuit, and the light bulb emits light. In this circuit all of the electrons continue to flow in the same direction. This is called *direct current (DC)*. Of course, if there's only one wire between the light bulb and the battery, or if there's an open switch, the circuit is incomplete. The electrons have to flow through a complete loop in order to make the bulb light.

Such is the case with all electrical circuits. There must be a complete loop providing both a place for electrons to come from and a place for them to go. This is why the plugs to all your appliances at home have two prongs. (*Note*: Some plugs have three prongs. The third is a safety ground prong.) Most electrical devices will also have a switch somewhere in the circuit to allow you to interrupt the flow of electrons.

### Alternating Current (AC)

The preceding example explained a simple DC circuit. Most circuits used in video equipment use direct current. However, there is another type of current that you will commonly encounter called *alternating current (AC)*. With AC the flow of electrons changes direction constantly. The current flows from negative to positive, then from positive to negative, and so on. AC is much more efficient for transmission through wires over long distances. That's one of the reasons that it is used for household electricity. Some household appliances work better on AC (e.g., your clothes washer), and others work better on DC (e.g., the internal circuits of your TV), so the ability to easily change AC into DC is another good reason we use AC power for our main electricity supply.

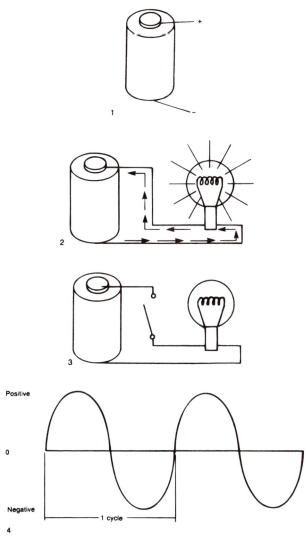

1. Battery (stored energy).

2. Simple circuit.

3. Simple circuit with switch.

4. Alternating current.

*When you're dealing with electricity, you need to be able to measure it.*

# Units of Measurement (1)

### Voltage
Several types of measurements relate to electricity. The first of these is voltage, which is measured in volts (V). *Voltage* is the pressure of the electricity. In a given medium, the speed of electricity is constant, but the pressure is not. The typical flashlight battery has a voltage of 1.5 V. The electricity in your home, on the other hand, is 120 V. So you could say that the electricity in your house has a lot more pressure behind it.

### Current
The second area of measurement for electricity is current, which is measured in amperes or amps (A). *Current* is the volume of electrons; that is, the number of electrons passing a certain point in a given time. A current of 4 amps has twice as many electrons passing by as does a current of 2 amps.

### Power
Voltage and current together determine power. *Power* is a measurement of work being accomplished and is measured in watts (W). Watts are determined by multiplying volts by amps. For example, if you have a light bulb that draws 1.25 amps and the house voltage is 120 V, your light bulb is a 150-W bulb (1.25 amps × 120 V = 150 W).

### Resistance
Another area of measurement is resistance. *Resistance* is the property of a material to "resist" the flow of electrons through it when voltage is applied. We measure this resistance in *ohms* (Ω).

### Mathematical Symbols and Formulas
Because they all concern the flow of electricity through a conductor, these basic units of measurement are all mathematically related. In addition, when working with units of measurement mathematically, we give them different symbols. The mathematical symbols and the basic formulas are shown in the table to the right. You may not need to memorize these formulas, but you should know that they exist and that the units are interrelated. It is also important to remember the different mathematical symbols.

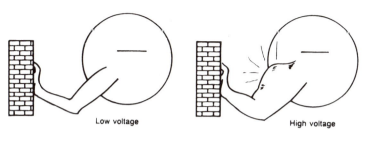

Low voltage    High voltage

1

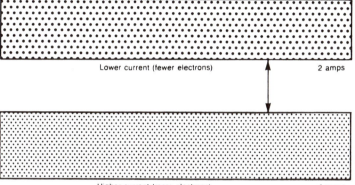

Lower current (fewer electrons)    2 amps

Higher current (more electrons)    4 amps

2

1. **Voltage.**

2. **Current.**

**Mathematical symbols and formulas.**

| Unit | Mathematical symbol | Basic formulas |
|------|---------------------|----------------|
| Watts | W | $E \times I$ or $I^2 \times R$ or $\dfrac{E^2}{R}$ |
| Volts | E | $I \times R$ or $W \times R$ or $\dfrac{W}{I}$ |
| Amperes | I | $\dfrac{E}{R}$ or $\dfrac{W}{R}$ or $\dfrac{W}{I}$ |
| Ohms | R | $\dfrac{E}{I}$ or $\dfrac{E^2}{W}$ or $\dfrac{W}{I^2}$ |

*These are also other measurements you need to know.*

# Units of Measurement (2)

Voltage, current, and resistance are basic measurements of electricity, but when you need to apply electricity to television, you will need to know some other measurements. Among these are frequency, hertz, and AC frequency.

### Frequency
*Frequency* is an action that repeats itself. If you have an electrical circuit that puts out repeated and equal bursts or pulses of energy at 100 of those pulses a second, the frequency of that circuit is 100 pulses per second. But we measure frequency in *hertz (Hz)*, so the frequency is 100 Hz.

### AC Frequency
In our earlier discussion of AC, you learned that the flow of electrons in AC current constantly changes direction. If the electricity in your home is 120 V AC, the electricity will go from 0 V up to +120 V, back down to 0 V, continue down to −120 V, and then go back up to 0 V. This alternation between 120 V of positive electricity and 120 V of negative electricity is one cycle. Your household electricity does this 60 times a second. So the frequency of your household electricity is 60 Hz. Thus, to be fully descriptive of the electricity in your house, you would say it's 120 V 60 Hz AC.

### Impedance
Just as DC circuits had resistance, AC circuits have impedance. *Impedance* is the combination of resistance, capacitance, and inductance (discussed later). Impedance can help tell the production person if two or more circuits will interact well. The following oversimplified example may help you understand the concept. If your stereo amplifier has a speaker impedance of 8 $\Omega$, this means that it is designed to hook up to speakers that have 8 $\Omega$ of resistance. If you connect your 8-$\Omega$ amplifier to your 8-$\Omega$ speakers, everything works great. But what happens when you connect that 8-$\Omega$ amplifier to speakers that have 10,000 $\Omega$ of resistance? Not much! The system just isn't designed to overcome that much resistance. On the other hand, if you have both an amplifier and speakers with 10,000 $\Omega$ of impedance, everything works just fine. But if you connect that 10,000-$\Omega$ amplifier to speakers that have 8-$\Omega$ resistance, you've got problems. You could destroy your speakers! They're just not designed to work with that amplifier. You have what's called a *mismatch*. Impedance is an important factor when integrating electrical components.

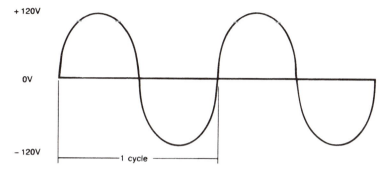

**Alternating current.**

# Fields (Induction) and Noise

### Fields (Induction)

Two other basic theories are necessary for understanding television equipment. The first of these is *fields* (induction). Any electrical circuit that has a changing flow of electrons will create an electromagnetic field around itself. For example, if you turned a flashlight on and off several times, the flow of electrons would be starting and stopping and a small electromagnetic field would be created. However, if you left the flashlight on, the flow of electrons would be continuous and unchanging and there would not be an electromagnetic field. Since the flashlight uses very small amounts of electricity, its field would be very small — almost unmeasurable. But a high-tension power line running cross-country has an extremely strong electromagnetic field. When another circuit is placed within this electromagnetic field, a signal from the more powerful circuit is forced, or coupled, into the weaker circuit. The signal may take the form of static, as when you try to play the AM radio in your car near high-power lines, or it may be actual information, as when you sometimes hear very weak background voices on the telephone.

### Noise

Another thing that can create problems is *noise*. To see what noise looks like in video, unhook the antenna and/or cable from your TV. Turn your TV on. What you see is noise! If you happen to be near a transmitter and have your TV tuned to its channel, you'll also see some picture. This noise is obviously an undesirable feature. Too much of it and it interferes with the picture or signal. Inherent in every electrical circuit is a certain amount of this noise. If there is too much noise, then there is a problem. Certainly, if you want to watch TV, you don't want to see any noise.

### Signal-to-Noise Ratio

You need to be able to measure the relationship between the strength of the signal and the amount of noise the circuitry creates. This measurement is called the *signal-to-noise ratio*. We use the decibel (dB) scale to measure this relationship. The dB scale is a logarithmic ratio. The signal-to-noise ratio is doubled for every 3-dB difference between the strength of the signal and the strength of the noise. For example, if the noise in our system is 0 dB and the signal is 3 dB, then the signal is twice as strong as the noise; if the signal is 6 dB, then it's four times as strong as the noise; if the signal is 9 dB, it's eight times as strong; 12 dB, 16 times as strong; 15 dB, 32 times as strong; and so on. In video, we like to have a signal-to-noise ratio of at least 60 dB.

**10**

**1. Induction.**

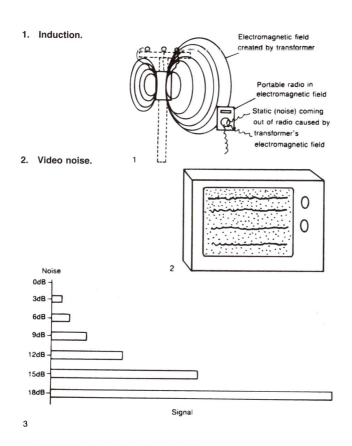

Electromagnetic field created by transformer

Portable radio in electromagnetic field

Static (noise) coming out of radio caused by transformer's electromagnetic field

**2. Video noise.**

1

2

Noise

3

Signal

+ 45-dB signal-to-noise ratio = signal is 45dB stronger than the noise

− 45-dB signal-to-noise ratio = noise is 45dB weaker than the signal

Therefore, + 45-dB signal-to-noise ratio = − 45-dB signal-to-noise ratio

4

**3. Signal-to-noise ratio. Comparison of the strength of the signal with the noise using the dB scale.**

**4. Minus and positive signal-to-noise ratios.**

*Now you need to learn some abbreviations that are frequently used.*

# Abbreviations

### Kilo

K is the abbreviation for *kilo*, which equals 1000. If something has a frequency of 10 KHz, it has a frequency of 10,000 Hz. You can just replace the word "thousand" with "kilo." Similarly, if you have a light in your TV studio that uses 1 KW of power, it is using 1000 W of power.

### Mega

M stands for *mega*, or 1,000,000. So a generator that puts out 1 MW of power gives 1,000,000 W of power. If your favorite radio station has an assigned frequency of 96 MHz, it has a frequency of 96,000,000 Hz.

### Giga

G stands for *giga* and is equal to 1,000,000,000. So a measurement of 6 GHz would be equal to 6,000,000,000 Hz.

K, M, and G are used for units that are greater than one. There are, however, several abbreviations that are used for measurements that are smaller than one.

### Milli

The first of these abbreviations is m, which stands for *milli* and means 1/1000. If you took a measurement and it read 5 mV, that is read as five millivolts or five one thousandths of a volt. A measurement of 321 mA would be read as 321 milliamps or 321 one thousandths of an amp.

### Micro

The next abbreviation is μ, which stands for *micro* and means 1/1,000,000. Thus, if you have a reading of 25 μsec, that is read as 25 microseconds or 25 one millionths of a second.

### Nano

The last abbreviation is n, which stands for *nano* and means 1/1,000,000,000. So a measurement of 63 nsec would be read as 63 one billionths of a second.

```
G = giga  =      1,000,000,000
M = mega  =          1,000,000
K = kilo  =              1,000
units     =                  1
m = milli =              1/1,000
μ = micro =          1/1,000,000
n = nano  =  1/1,000,000,000
```

1

Smaller to larger, decimal point goes left.

Larger to smaller, decimal point goes right.

The difference in the number of zeros determines the number of spaces the decimal point is moved.

2

1.  Chart of abbreviations.

2.  Rules of conversion.

# Cathode Ray Tubes (CRTs)

The television picture tube that displays the picture is properly called a *cathode ray tube (CRT)*. The CRT is a large glass vacuum tube. The inside front of the tube is covered with a phosphorescent substance that glows when struck by a beam of electrons — the stronger the beam of electrons, the brighter the glow; the weaker the electron beam, the less the glow. At the back of the CRT, in the narrow neck, is an electron gun (a cathode that is heated) that emits a beam of electrons — the higher the voltage activating the gun, the stronger the electron beam; the weaker the voltage, the weaker the beam. The direction of the electron beam is controlled by the deflection yoke (a group of large electromagnets surrounding the middle section of the CRT).

### Interlace Scanning
Since a beam of electrons isn't very wide, one horizontal sweep across the CRT doesn't give us much information. To get more information, the electron beam has to go back and make successive horizontal sweeps of the CRT. In the U.S. system, it makes 525 sweeps, or lines, top to bottom, to cover the entire face of the CRT. But things aren't quite that simple. Rather than just sweeping all 525 lines at once, the system goes through and sweeps the odd lines (line numbers 1, 3, 5, 7, 9, . . .) first and then goes back and sweeps the even lines (line numbers 2, 4, 6, 8, . . .). Thus, we have two separate fields of 262.5 lines each. When these two fields are combined, they give us our single video frame or a complete picture of 525 lines. This will give us 60 fields and 30 frames every second. This process is called *interlace scanning*, and the reason for it will be explained a little later.

### Progressive Scanning
Computers and some formats of digital television use progressive scanning. In *progressive scanning* there are no interlaced fields. Each frame is scanned line by line in progressive (1, 2, 3, 4, 5, 6, . . .) order from top to bottom. Since computers don't have the bandwidth limitations (see the next section) of broadcast, they move in the direction of progressive scanning. (In the very earliest days of home computing, some computers used the home TV as the computer monitor and so used interlace scanning. As home computing advanced, the quality of picture that the computer produced exceeded what a TV set could show.)

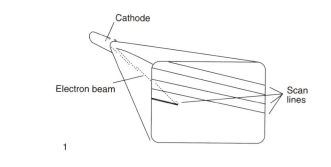

Cathode

Electron beam

Scan lines

1

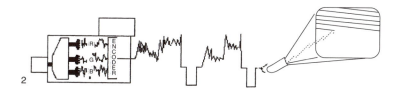

R
G
B

ENCODER

2

1. CRT.

2. Analog video system.

*The CRT converts the video signal into visual images.*

## Need for Interlace Scanning

This is a convenient time to explain why the interlace scanning method is used in the NTSC (National Television System Committee) television system. Our TV system was developed over 50 years ago. Engineers had to work within the limitations of the time. One of those limitations was the phosphor coating of the CRTs. When the CRT's electron beam struck a phosphor on the face plate, it caused that phosphor to glow. As soon as the electron beam left the phosphor, the glow started to get weaker. If our CRT scanned from line 1 all the way down to line 525 in succession, by the time the electron beam got to the bottom of the picture, the top of the picture would be pretty dark. To prevent this effect, the electron beam scans a field of 262.5 lines and then goes back to the top of the picture. Just as the lines at the top start to darken, the electron beam fills in the spaces between the darkening lines with bright new information. As a result, the overall picture maintains an even brightness. So, the *interlace scanning* system is the method used to ensure that the picture has an even brightness throughout instead of having separate bright and dark bands.

In addition, there is only so much room for information. This limitation is called *bandwidth*. You might think of it as how many lanes there are on the highway or how big the water pipe is. The highway and pipe determine how many cars or how much water can be carried. In the TV signal, if we tried to scan 525 lines in sequence one after the other (line numbers 1, 2, 3, 4, 5, 6, ...) for 60 frames, it would take more bandwidth than was available. With today's technology it is possible to design systems that scan lines in this way. This type of scanning is called *progressive scanning*. In fact, engineers would prefer to do this because it eliminates some problems created by interlace scanning. However, all current TV sets would be incompatible with such a system. As a result, we still use interlace scanning. This will change in the future. New technologies to be discussed later in this book will allow TV sets to display either interlace or progressive scanning.

1

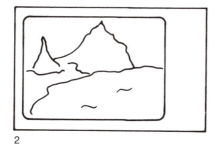

2

1. TV without interlace scanning.

2. TV with interlace scanning.

**17**

*The electron beam needs to get back to its starting point.*

# Blanking

The intensity of the electron beam during the scanning process is not constant. It varies in a logical, consistent pattern corresponding with the brightness of the picture as the beam moves across and up and down the CRT's face. If the electron beam were at full power when it returned to the beginning of a new line or field, it would illuminate phosphors on the CRT face and interfere with the information previously laid down. In order to prevent this from happening, the electron beam is turned down to a very low power so that it can return to the beginning of a new line or field. This period of time when the electron beam is turned down is called *blanking*.

### Horizontal Blanking
In the scanning process, the electron beam scans the CRT, laying down the first line of information. When the beam reaches the edge of the area defining the TV screen, it is turned down to a low voltage, although it continues for a moment in the same direction. When the beam reaches the edge of the CRT, it quickly reverses direction and returns to the other side of the screen. Once it reaches the other side, the beam resumes its original direction. Its voltage is then turned back up to lay down another line. This process occurs every time lines are scanned.

The duration of the lowered voltage, from the end of one line to the beginning of the next, is called *horizontal blanking*. During this horizontal blanking period, the return of the electron beam from one side of the CRT to the other is called *retrace*.

### Vertical Blanking
You've seen what happens at the end of each line. Something similar happens at the end of each field. After laying down a field of information, the electron beam is turned down to a low voltage before it retraces back to the top of the image. Once in position at the top of the screen, the beam's voltage is turned back up and it starts scanning a new field. The time that the beam's voltage is turned down until it is turned back up again is called *vertical blanking* or the *vertical interval*. When the electron beam is retracing back to the beginning of a new field, it's called *vertical sync*.

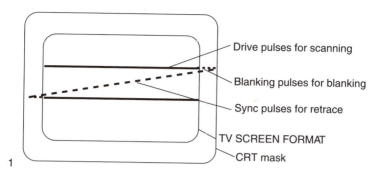

Drive pulses for scanning

Blanking pulses for blanking

Sync pulses for retrace

TV SCREEN FORMAT

CRT mask

1

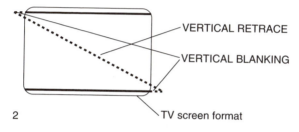

VERTICAL RETRACE

VERTICAL BLANKING

TV screen format

2

1. **Parts of the TV picture.**
2. **Vertical blanking.**

# Waveform Display

The horizontal scanning movement of the electron beam can be diagrammed another way. Take a look at the figure at the right. This graph represents an electron beam scanning one line of information, returning to the other side of the target during blanking, and reading a new line of video. Everything above the base line represents the electron beam sweeping across the target in its normal direction, collecting information; anything below the base line is the beam returning in the other direction.

The graph actually measures the voltage of the electron beam in special units called IRE units (for Institute of Radio Engineers, now called the Institute of Electrical and Electronics Engineers). The baseline is 0 unit, which is simply 0 voltage. Notice that the height of the graph ranges from 100 to about −40 IRE. Just above the baseline the black portions of the picture are registered. This area near the baseline where the black portions of the picture appear is called the *pedestal.*

Above the baseline, 100 IRE units indicate the maximum voltage the video system can handle and still provide a good picture. Information located here is called the *white peak.* Moving from left to right on this diagram, we see that the voltages vary a great deal. As discussed earlier, the higher voltages are the bright parts of the picture, and the lower voltages are the darker parts. Then there is a flat line of very little voltage; this is the start of blanking. The blanking continues for a little way and then suddenly drops below the baseline; this is the start of retrace. After retrace, the voltage rises back above the baseline and remains at this low level until a new video line begins.

When you walk around the equipment area of a TV studio, you'll see several displays, like the one just discussed. These are waveform displays, and they're very important to both production people and engineers. The waveform monitor, which shows these displays, provides a graphic display of the black and white portion of the picture. The voltage signal generated from the black and white portion of the picture, its brightness, is also called the picture's *luminance.*

When shown on the waveform monitor, however, the blanking and retrace are known by different names. The retrace is called the *sync*, *sync pulse*, or *horizontal sync*; in fact, it's hardly ever called retrace around the studio. Two other parts of the blanking also pick up new names. The first part of the blanking is called the *front porch*, and the last part of the blanking is called the *back porch.*

**20**

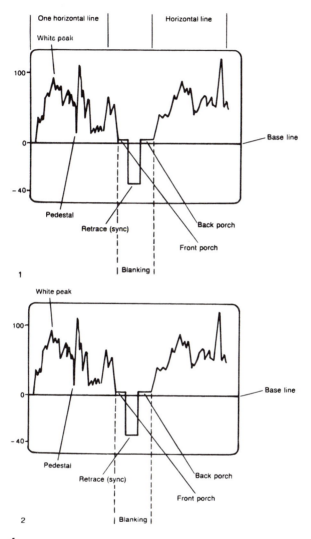

1. Waveform scan.

2. Waveform monitor continuously displaying the scanning of CRT by the electron beam.

**21**

# Charge-Coupled Devices

*Charge-coupled devices (CCDs)* are the parts inside of the camera that change the light focused on them by the camera lens into electrical signals. CCDs have been developed from the same sort of solid-state silicon chip technology that has made computers faster, smaller, more powerful, and cheaper; put powerful radios into small packages; and made home camcorders the size of a book.

## CCD Layout and Operation

These chips are laid out with rows of photosensitive elements; these are our picture elements (pixels). The number of pixels on a CCD is defined by its matrix. For example, a matrix of 704 × 480 would indicate that there are 704 pixels placed across the screen horizontally in each of 480 vertical rows. This would give a total of 337,920 pixels in the picture. When light hits one of these pixels, a distinct electrical voltage is created. The brighter the light, the higher the voltage; the darker the light, the lower the voltage. All of these discrete voltages are read off left to right and top to bottom into a memory. The memory is then fed out, horizontal line by horizontal line, in sync with the rest of the system. Once the face of the CCD has been cleared, a new image forms and the process is repeated.

## Broadcast-Quality Requirements

To meet broadcast-quality standards, a CCD needs to have a minimum of 330,000 pixels. Since having more pixels gives higher detail and resolution, it would be nice to have even more than that. Cramming that many pixels into an area a little larger than your thumbnail has been a major problem. It took engineers more than 10 years to solve the problems, but they have been very successful and CCD cameras are now the standard of the industry.

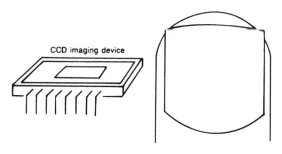

1. CCD next to a thumb; the scale is roughly accurate.

2. CCD layout. This diagram shows horizontal and vertical layout of a CCD. Each dot represents a distinct picture element.

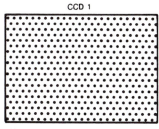

CCD 1

Not enough pixels for broadcast quality

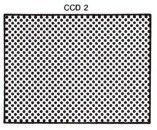

CCD 2

Approaching broadcast quality density

3. Broadcast-quality CCDs need a high pixel density.

4. In the past, CCDs were expensive because each batch produced only a small number of usable chips.

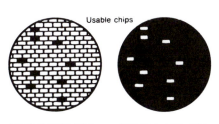

Usable chips

Low % of usable chips          High % of usable chips

# An Introduction to Digital (1)

### What Is Digital?

What we have been discussing up to now is called *analog video*. In the analog process, the bright images on the face of the CCD are changed into higher voltages, and the darker images on the CCD are turned into lower voltages. These are then reproduced on the CRT where the higher voltages create brighter images and the lower voltages create darker images. This process has been around for more than 60 years. But the analog process has a lot of problems. The quality of the picture is limited and can easily be degraded by some equipment. If we could move into the world of computers, we could improve the quality of the picture, maintain that quality throughout the process, and create images and effects that can otherwise only be "seen" in the mind's eye. This is what digital video does. *Digital video* is a process that uses computer technology and language to create, store, and transmit video images.

### What Computers Do

Computers are really very stupid machines. They can only do what we tell them to do and how we tell them to do it. The real brilliance of these machines comes from the men and women who design the internal electronics and who write the software programs that tell the machines how to make those designs work. If you have a basic understanding of what computers deal with, you will have a better appreciation of the people who create and program these machines.

Computers can only do one thing: manipulate numbers; they are number crunchers, calculators. But they can't even handle the numbers 1 through 10 in the same way that you and I can. When you get down to the smallest, tiniest part of the computer's memory, it can only deal with one of two things, as discussed next.

Analog is a constantly changing stream of voltages.

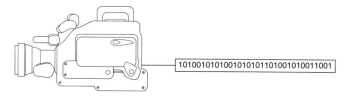

1010010101001010101101001010011001

Digital is a constant stream of numbers.

*A computer can only deal with one of two values.*

# An Introduction to Digital (2)

### Bits and Bytes — Binary Numbering System

The smallest part of the computer's memory is called a *bit*. It either has an electrical charge or it doesn't. If the bit has no charge, it is represented by the number 0; if the bit has a charge it is represented by the number 1. That's it! That's all computers can deal with: 0s and 1s. As you can see, a 0 or a 1 isn't much information. So in order to have a segment of memory that we can use effectively, we have to combine numbers of bits together into a unit that is called a *byte*. In 8-bit processing we would combine 8 bits. In 10-bit processing we could combine 10 bits and so on.

Let's look at 8-bit processing since that is what is used in the home computers familiar to you. Since each bit has only two possibilities, 0 or 1, when we combine two bits together we have four possibilities: 00, 01, 10, or 11. When we combine 8 bits together, we have 256 possibilities ($2^8$ or 2 multiplied by itself 8 times: $2 \times 2 \times 2 \times 2 \times 2 \times 2 \times 2 \times 2 = 256$). With 10-bit processing you would add 2 more bits to the process and get 1024 possible combinations. With the 256 combinations of 8-bit processing, we can assign one specific combination to represent the capital letter "A" and a different specific combination to represent the small letter "a." We can do the same thing for the letters "B," "C," "D," and so on. We can also use specific combinations to represent punctuation marks, the numbers 0 through 9, mathematical symbols, and so on. The software, the computer's program, tells the computer how to use that information. "Treat this specific byte combination like it is the letter 'A' in the alphabet." The byte, then, is the smallest segment of memory that can be used as a piece of information: a letter or a digit or a punctuation mark or such.

So no matter what a computer may seem to be doing — surfing the web, writing a paper for class, or creating wild video images — what it is really doing is manipulating numbers (0s and 1s).

**1. Bits.**                                                    00 01 10 11

                                                                   1

**2. Bytes (8-bit processing).**   | 10001101 | 11000101 | 01010111 | 10101101 |

                                    2

*Digital technology can solve many video problems.*

# Analog and Digital

### A to D Conversion

Changing the signal from analog voltages into a stream of numbers for digital video takes place in a device known as an *analog-to-digital (A to D) converter*.

The video signal, from 0 to 100 on the waveform monitor, is approximately 0.7 V strong. You know that the stronger the voltage (0.7), the brighter the glow on the CRT; the weaker the voltage (0.0), the darker the CRT. If we pick a point right in the middle of that range (0.35 V), we could probably figure out that would be in the middle of the gray range. This is sort of what the A to D converter does. The brightness range is divided into 256 possible levels (8-bit processing), with 0.00 V equaling the 0 level and 0.7 V equaling 255. Midway through the voltage range (0.35 V) would also be midway through the number range (127). As a result each of the 256 numbers represents a separate and distinct voltage and brightness. (Remember, these voltages have been rounded off.)

### Sampling and Quantizing

The process of grabbing a piece of the video information and holding it is called *sampling*; the process of changing that sample into a number is called *quantizing*. How often a sample is taken is very important. If we sampled the video only a few times a line, we wouldn't get a very accurate picture of what was happening. If you think of the brightness levels along one axis and the sample points along the other axis, you can turn the waveform display into a point-by-point graph that is quite representative. That has been done in the illustration on the right. Imagine how much more accurate it would be with several hundred sampling points instead of a few. The more times we sample a line of video, the more accurate will be our digital representation of that line. Quantizing is the process of turning the individual sample points into numbers.

### D to A Conversion

To display a picture, the stream of digital information (numbers) must be converted back to a stream of analog voltages. This is necessary so that the electron gun at the back of the CRT can shoot a stream of electrons to spray the picture onto the phosphors on the face of the CRT. This takes place in the *digital-to-analog (D to A) converter*. Since each number in the digital stream represents a specific voltage, the D to A converter takes the right amount of voltage from the wall outlet and replaces the numbers with that voltage. As a result, a stream of numbers enters the D to A converter and a stream of voltages leaves it.

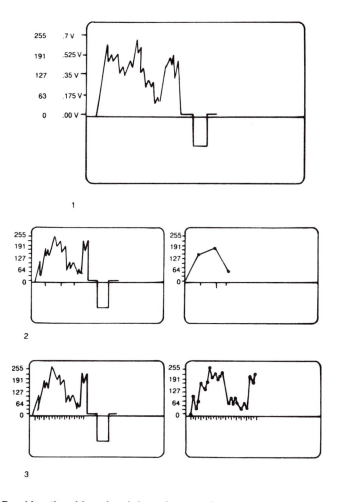

1. Breaking the video signal down into numbers.

2. Sampling only a few times a line.

3. Sampling several times a line.

*The color system is similar to black and white but is more complex.*

# Color Systems

### Color versus Black and White

You've been shown how a visual image is created on a CCD, converted to an analog video signal, and transferred to a CRT for display. Black and white video systems operate this way. A black and white camera, if one were made today, would have one CCD and only black and white information; that is, luminance would be created and conveyed to the CRT. Color video is based on these same basic principles but is a little more complex.

### Additive and Subtractive Colors

Instead of having just one CCD, high-quality color cameras have three CCDs, one for each of the primary colors: red, green, and blue. Those of you who have had art classes might say, "Now wait a minute, the primary colors are red, blue, and yellow." Well, you're right, if you're dealing with subtractive colors. Subtractive colors are what you deal with if you're mixing paints; subtractive colors reflect light off themselves. In painting, you start with a white canvas and add colors. To get to white you have to subtract the colors until you get to the white canvas. Thus you have *subtractive colors*. In video, we're dealing with *additive colors*. Unlike subtractive colors, which depend on substances that interact with white light, additive colors depend on the color of the light itself. In this case the absence of colors gives you black. If you add all of the primary colors together, you get white. These are additive colors. With additive colors, the primaries are red, green, and blue.

### Complementary Colors

You can see by the figure at the right that by mixing what appears to be equal parts of any two primary additive colors you will get one of the *complementary colors*. That is, equal parts of red and green will produce yellow, red and blue will produce magenta, and blue and green will produce cyan. When all three primary colors are mixed together, we have white light. By changing the proportions of the mix, brightness (intensity), and saturation of the colors, an infinite number of colors in the visible spectrum can be produced.

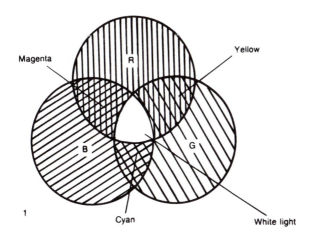

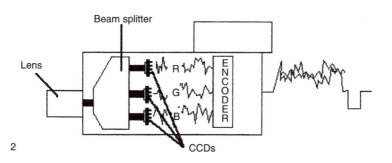

1. **TV colors.**

2. **Color TV camera.**

# How the Eye Sees Light (1)

In the section on complementary colors it was indicated that a mix of equal parts of red, blue, and green light would produce white light. In reality white light is 59% green, 30% red, and 11% blue. How is this contradiction explained? It isn't really a contradiction. Your eyes are not equally sensitive to all colors of light. What looks like equal amounts of red, green, and blue aren't really equal amounts at all. The CCDs, however, are equally sensitive to all colors of light. For your eyes to see white on the television screen, the TV camera must produce a picture that is 59% green, 30% red, and 11% blue.

### Color Temperature

If you've ever taken photographs outside and then gone indoors and taken more pictures without using a flash, you've gotten some disappointing results. Chances are that the pictures taken outside looked great, but those taken indoors had an orange/yellow cast to them. What you've seen is the result of the difference of color temperature. *Color temperature* is a way of measuring the color characteristics of light. Color temperature has nothing to do with heat or cold. The higher the color temperature, the more blue there is in the light. The lower the color temperature, the more orange there is in the light. The light outside on a bright, sunny day might be around 5600° K (Kelvin, the scale used to measure color temperature). The light in your home is probably around 2600° K. This is why the colors in the photographs look so different. If you use a flash indoors, the light will be the same color temperature as daylight and your photographs will look fine. You don't see the change in color temperature because your eyes and brain compensate for you. If you see a person in a yellow jacket outdoors and then the two of you go indoors, your brain knows that it's the same jacket and it couldn't have changed colors. Your brain sees the jacket as the same color. A camera can't do that.

| | | |
|---|---|---|
| Overcast sky | 7,000 K | Blue |
| Noon daylight | 5,000 K | |
| TV studio lights | 3,200 K | |
| Household lights | 2,600 K | |
| Sunrise/sunset | 2,500 K | |
| Candle | 1,900 K | Orange |

1

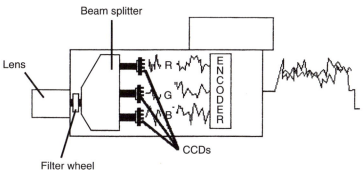

2

1. Approximate color temperature of some common light sources.

2. Color TV camera, showing location of filter wheel.

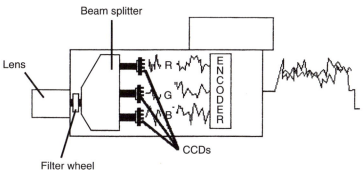

# How the Eye Sees Light (2)

Since the camera doesn't have a brain, it needs help to compensate for color temperature changes.

### Filters

One thing a camera can do to compensate for changes in color temperature is to use *filters*. Most cameras have a built-in filter wheel. This is a device that will allow you to place one of several filters between the lens of the camera and the beam splitter. Most cameras are set up to operate with TV studio lights, which have a color temperature of 3200° K. If you go outdoors to shoot, you will change the filter wheel to compensate for the change of color temperature.

### Black Balance

Changing the filter wheel is only the first step. Because clouds, shade, reflections, and other conditions all have an effect on color temperature, you will have to balance your camera every time you set it up in new lighting conditions, which is simply establishing the proper color combination for given lighting conditions. The first step is to *black balance* the camera. Black balance ensures that there is no color information and that each of the color channels is set at 7.5 (for NTSC, 0 for PAL). The next step is to white balance the camera.

### White Balance

To *white balance* a camera, simply aim and focus it on a white card and push the white balance button. The electronic circuitry of the camera will then adjust its light reception so that the green CCD produces 59% of the picture, the red CCD produces 30%, and the blue CCD produces 11% (see previous discussion). Since the camera is now properly mixing the three primary colors, the rest of the color spectrum will be fine.

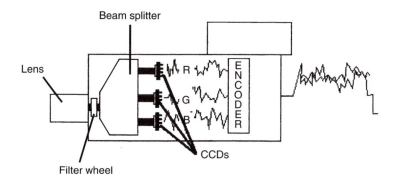

**Color TV camera, showing location of filter wheel.**

*Encoding more information produces better pictures.*

# Digital Encoding Ratios

### From Black and White to Color

When color television was finally adopted in the United States in 1953, black and white TV had already been around for several years. To ensure that the black and white TVs and the new color TVs could show all of the same programs, engineers decided to start with the black and white signal and add the color information to it. The black and white or luminance signal is designated as "Y." Since each of the three primary colors contains luminance information, it would be redundant and use too much bandwidth to have a separate luminance signal and three separate color or chrominance signals. The solution is to take the Y channel for luminance, which is mostly green information (since green makes 59% of white light), and two color signals: red with the luminance information removed (R-Y) and blue with the luminance information removed (B-Y). This allows recreation of the full color picture without using more bandwidth than is necessary.

### Digital Responses to This Situation

When developing a digital system, engineers have to make choices about how accurately they want to reproduce the picture and how much bandwidth they want to use. One choice they make is with digital encoding ratios. A *digital encoding ratio* is the relationship of how much luminance and how much chrominance information are encoded digitally. The international broadcast standard is 4:2:2. What that means is that if we were to take four pixels from the TV screen, all four of them would have the Y or luminance information encoded, and two of the pixels would have the R-Y information and the B-Y information encoded. If we had 4:1:1 encoding, which some companies use in consumer color cameras, then all four pixels would have the luminance information encoded, and one would have both the R-Y and B-Y information encoded.

Obviously, the more information that is encoded, the more accurate the picture. But you will use more bandwidth and will pay more money for the better quality. A problem is created, however, when you try to use several pieces of digital equipment together. If one has 4:2:2 encoding and you try to hook it up to something that has 4:1:1 encoding, it probably won't work. The equipment may have built-in converters, but when you constantly convert from one digital format to another, you begin to lose quality. It is critical that you and your engineering staff ensure that all digital equipment in a facility is compatible with each other.

**36**

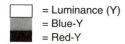
= Luminance (Y)
= Blue-Y
= Red-Y

PIXELS

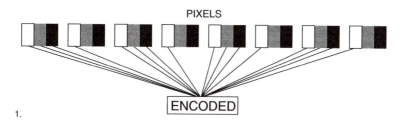

ENCODED

1.

PIXELS

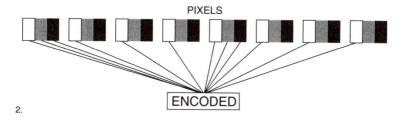

ENCODED

2.

1. 4:2:2 encoding.

2. 4:1:1 encoding.

**37**

*Digital equipment must be able to talk to each other.*

# CODECs

The word *CODEC* stands for CODe/DECode. A CODEC defines a digital standard. It will include sampling frequency, processing level, encoding ratios, compression standards (to be discussed later in this book), and other information.

Most digital equipment will produce both analog and digital outputs. If you hook up the analog output of one piece of digital equipment to the analog input of another piece of equipment, they will "talk to each other," but it is complicated. In the first piece of equipment, the digital signal will go through a D to A converter to become analog. As soon as it is in the next piece of equipment, it must go through an A to D converter to become digital. It would be much simpler to go directly from digital out to digital in. The CODEC will tell you if this is possible. If two pieces of equipment use the same CODEC, they will talk to each other digitally. If the equipment uses different CODECs, they will not talk to each other digitally and you will have to use the analog connections.

Obviously then, when buying equipment or putting together a studio, you want to buy digital equipment that can all use the same CODEC. That way everything can remain in digital form throughout.

Many digital formats are available, so ensuring that everything you buy uses the same CODEC is critical.

When CODECs match, digital equipment can talk to each other digitally.

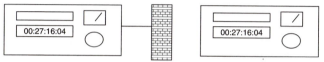

When CODECs are not the same, digital equipment cannot talk to each other digitally.

*Encoding combines many signals into one.*

## Composite Encoding

The process of combining the three color signals is called *encoding*. The encoded signal, now called a *composite signal*, actually comprises two parts — the *chroma* (color) signal and the *luminance* (brightness) signal. Although there is some variation, the separate luminance signal is formed by skimming brightness information from each of the three CCDs. It is then recombined with the chroma signal to create the composite signal. If you had only a black and white TV, you would receive and watch only the luminance signal. The encoded, composite signal is fed out the back of the camera. The color TV has a decoder built in to re-create the three separate R, G, B signals.

### Home Video Cameras

Note that some color home video cameras use only one chip instead of three. These chips have a filter of colored stripes in front of them. This striped filter breaks up the light into the three primary colors. Circuitry in the camera then combines these stripes of color into a composite color picture. As a result of this process, these cameras seldom approach broadcast quality. They rarely have the picture sharpness or color saturation needed for professional work. Even home video cameras that have three chips are of poorer quality than professional cameras. The chips they use have fewer pixels and are not of the same quality as those used in professional cameras.

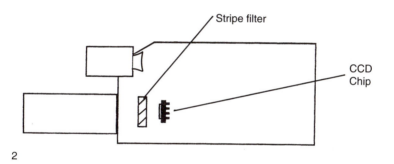

Luminance information

R

G

B

ENCODER

Encoded composite video signal

Chrominance information

1

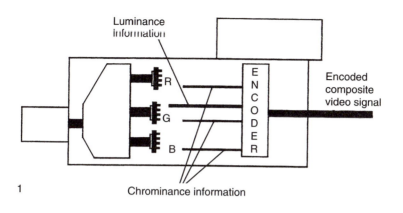

Stripe filter

CCD Chip

2

1. **Encoding.**

2. **Color home video camera.**

# Color CRTs

Just as the color camera works in a manner similar to the black and white camera, the color CRT works in a manner similar to the black and white CRT. The color CRT has three sets of color phosphor dots laid down on the inside of the CRT. These are laid down in a specific pattern. The exact pattern will differ from manufacturer to manufacturer, but for the sake of explanation, a very common pattern, the triad, will be used. As you can see from the first figure on the right, the triad is made up of one red phosphor dot, one green phosphor dot, and one blue phosphor dot arranged in a triangular pattern.

At the back of the CRT there are three separate electron guns, one each for the red, green, and blue information. Close to the front of the tube is a thin metal mask. This mask has tiny holes in it, arranged in such a way that only the red electron beam can strike a red phosphor, the green beam a green phosphor, and the blue beam a blue phosphor. These phosphors are so small and close together that they can't be seen as separate and distinct unless they are looked at under magnification. Thus, when they are struck by the electron beams, their colors blend together to produce the same color that the camera split up. The red part of a stop sign, for example, would cause only the corresponding red phosphors to be illuminated, while the white letters of the sign would cause all of those corresponding phosphors to glow.

### Convergence

The CRT can experience a problem called *convergence*. If you look at the diagram on the right, you will see that each of the electron guns at the back of the CRT is a different distance from the phosphors. The gun that is mounted at the lowest place in the CRT neck will be farther from the phosphors at the top of the screen than the gun that is mounted at the top of the neck of the CRT. Since the electrons travel at a constant speed, the electrons that have to travel a longer distance will arrive at the phosphors an instant later than electrons from the other guns. This is the convergence problem.

If there is a convergence problem, we could see up to three distinct offset images of different colors. Convergence shouldn't be a problem with most home TVs, but it can be with some large-screen projection units. You can usually make some control adjustments to lessen or minimize convergence problems.

We can see from this discussion that the color video system is considerably more complex than the black and white system. In fact, the color camera might be thought of as three synchronized cameras and the color CRT as three separate CRTs synchronized together.

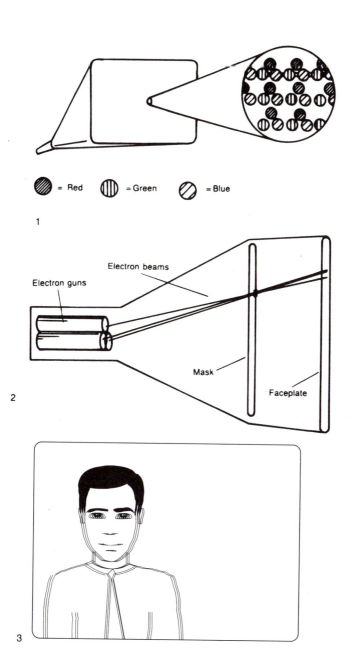

= Red    = Green    = Blue

1

Electron beams

Electron guns

Mask

Faceplate

2

3

1. Color CRT.
2. Components of a color CRT.
3. CRT convergence error.

**43**

# Plasma Display Screen

There is a limit to how large you can make a CRT. As the CRT gets larger and larger, the glass enclosure must get thicker and thicker to maintain strength; this adds a lot of weight to an already heavy set. A new kind of screen is available for showing video that gives a larger viewing area without the size and weight problems of the very large CRTs. The device is only about 4 to 5 inches thick and is sometimes called a *flat-screen display*, although the proper name is *plasma display screen* or *device*.

The plasma display screen is made up of two pieces of glass sandwiched together. The back part has ridges going vertically down the glass. In the space between the ridges, alternating columns of red, green, and blue phosphors are laid down. For each color of each pixel there is an electrode on the back that is called the *data electrode*. The front piece of glass has horizontal ridges across it that will seal off each pixel from the others. The front panel also has two transparent electrodes for each pixel color: a *scan electrode* and a *common electrode*. When the front and back panels are sandwiched together, rare gases (helium, neon, and xenon) are trapped within the pixel compartments. So if we were to look at an individual pixel of the plasma display screen, there would be a red compartment with a trapped rare gas that has a data electrode on the back and transparent scan and common electrodes on the front. There would be a green and a blue compartment set up the same way. The three compartments together would make one pixel.

## How It Works

To activate a color of a pixel, an electrical charge is sent to the scan and data electrodes on the front and back of the screen. This charge electrifies the rare gas inside the pixel segment. A gas with an electrical charge is called a *plasma*, which is the source of the name for the screen. The plasma gives off an invisible ultraviolet light that causes the phosphor to glow. The phosphor will continue to glow as long as the charge is held and the plasma is active. To turn off the phosphor, the charge is drained off through the common electrode. When the charge is drained, the plasma returns to its uncharged, nonplasma, inactive gas state and the phosphor stops glowing. By activating individual pixel colors and varying the time each color is charged, a full range of colors can be created. Since the color is either on or off and varying voltages are not used, the plasma screen is a digital device.

Besides being only 4 or 5 inches thick, being able to be hung on a wall, and having a very large viewing area, these displays have an excellent contrast range and present very bright pictures. The prices have come down dramatically in the last few years and are now affordable to many people.

**44**

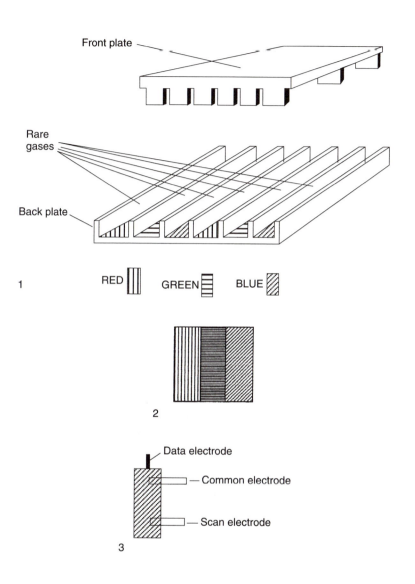

Front plate

Rare gases

Back plate

1

RED    GREEN    BLUE

2

Data electrode
— Common electrode
— Scan electrode

3

1. **Plasma display screen.**

2. **Individual pixel.**

3. **Pixel element.**

*There is another type of flat screen that is often used with computers.*

# LCD Screens

*LCD* stands for liquid crystal display. LCD screens are very complex; this description is therefore going to be very simplified and leave a lot out. The important thing is that you understand the concept of how these screens work.

LCD is an unusual substance that has traits of both liquids and solids. The key aspect for us is that when a voltage is applied to the liquid crystal, the crystal part turns within the liquid. An LCD screen is made up of many layers sandwiched together. Among the layers will be a filter layer that has red, green, and blue filters for each pixel element. Then will come a layer of glass that has a transparent contact for each pixel element's color. Then will come the liquid crystal substance. Next will be another glass layer with a transparent contact for each pixel element's color. Finally, there will be a light source — often a fluorescent light.

In their normal state, the liquid crystal elements will be flat so that no light can get past them to the colored filters. When an electrical charge is run through them from the glass plate in front to the glass plate behind them, it causes the crystal elements to rotate onto their edges, allowing the light behind them to pass through to the colored filter in front of them. Controlling the electrical charge controls how much the crystals rotate and how much light gets past them. This is how the mix of red, green, and blue is controlled to give us the whole range of colors that we see.

At the time of this writing, LCDs are used for small to medium-sized displays. There are many technical difficulties in producing quality LCD screens as large as some of the current plasma screens. LCD screens are also more expensive than plasma screens of the same size. Engineers are working hard to solve these problems so that one day soon large, high-quality LCD screens will provide the best quality for large-screen viewing. At that time we will be saying goodbye to CRTs and plasma. Both plasma and LCDs provide better pictures that will take up less space in our rooms. CRTs have served us well for the last 60 years, but their days are numbered.

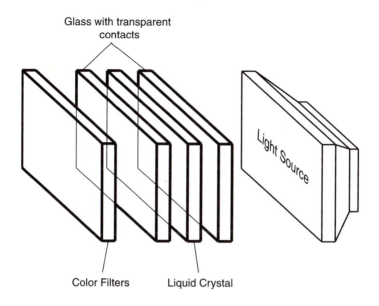

Glass with transparent contacts

Light Source

Color Filters    Liquid Crystal

LCD screens are made up of many layers.

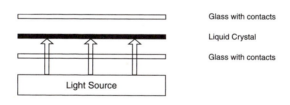

Glass with contacts

Liquid Crystal

Glass with contacts

Light Source

Liquid crystal at rest blocks light from passing through.

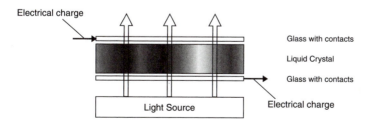

Electrical charge

Glass with contacts

Liquid Crystal

Glass with contacts

Light Source

Electrical charge

Liquid crystal with an electrical charge lets light pass through.

*The system needs to have a standard beat.*

# Analog Sync Generators

What exactly is a sync generator? A descriptive name would be color synchronizing pulse-generating system. No wonder that it is simply called a *sync generator*. The sync generator is the master clock that coordinates the whole system. Like a drummer in a band, it sets the rhythm that keeps everything in time and running together as a unit rather than as a bunch of individual components, each doing its own thing. When you're working with a single camera, it's not that big a job, but when you start developing a more complex system, the job becomes more difficult.

Imagine that you have two separate cameras working independently of each other. You turn their power on, and off they go. The fact that their CCDs are scanning different parts of their targets at the same instant in time (out of sync or nonsynchronous) is no big deal. But what happens if we try to hook those cameras together through a switcher (a device that allows you to instantaneously change between different video sources)? In the diagram at the right, the electron guns of each CRT are in different locations scanning their targets. Assume that camera 1 is being shown on the program monitor (the monitor that shows what is being recorded or transmitted). What happens if you try to make an instantaneous change (cut) to camera 2? Since the cameras are out of sync, the picture on the program monitor will roll, jump, flicker, or tear — a so-called glitch. In other words, there will be a major picture disruption or breakup when the cut is made.

Imagine, on the other hand, what would happen if the electron guns on the two cameras had been scanning together. Depending on the switcher, there might still be a breakup, but it would be less severe. The sync generator is the remedy to this problem. Each of the cameras is sent a synchronizing signal, which keeps the cameras scanning together so that you can make clean transitions between cameras.

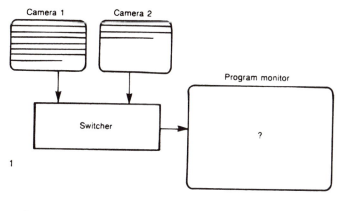

1

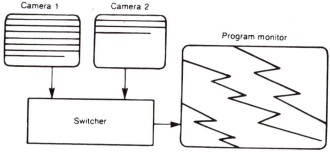

2

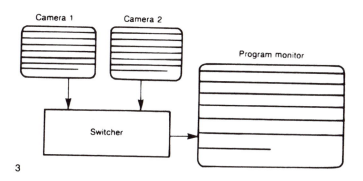

3

1. An unsynchronized system.

2. Making a transition with an unsynchronized system.

3. Making a transition with a synchronized system.

*Every picture needs certain information.*

# Analog Sync Generator Signals (1)

## Drive Pulses

The first thing the sync generator provides is *drive pulses*. These are the signals that tell the camera what line of the CCD to read off. There are two types of drive pulses, one each to control both the horizontal and vertical position of information being read off of the CCD. These two types are horizontal drive pulses and vertical drive pulses.

## Blanking Pulses

The second type of signal the sync generator provides is *blanking pulses*. As you might suspect, the blanking pulses tell the electron gun when to lower its voltage at the end of a line or field. There are two types of blanking pulses: horizontal blanking pulses (end of a line) and vertical blanking pulses (end of a field).

## Sync Pulses

The third type of signal the sync generator provides is *sync pulses*. Horizontal sync pulses tell the electron gun to retrace to the beginning of the next line. Vertical sync pulses are at the end of a field and tell the electron gun to retrace to the top of the picture. The third type of sync pulse that the sync generator generates is *color sync*, also called color subcarrier, color burst, or 3.58 (pronounced "three five eight," the meaning of which will be explained later on this page).

## Color Burst

*Color burst*, the fourth type of signal, is a reference signal inserted in the back porch of every line of video. The color burst acts as a marker, and the color information for each line is encoded onto that line based on the marker. If the marker is off, so is the color. The key aspect of that marker is its frequency. The color burst is really a burst of energy at a specific frequency. That frequency is 3,579,545 Hz $\pm$ 5 Hz. This is normally rounded up to 3.58 MHz, hence the name 3.58. (PAL systems use a color burst frequency of 4.4 Mhz.) If that frequency is off, the colors will be off.

Rather than sending all of these sync signals separately to each device in a television system, which requires a lot of additional cables and connectors, the television industry has developed a combined signal called *color black reference* or *black reference* or just *black*. This reference signal, which is delivered on one cable, contains all of the necessary sync signals for color television system synchronization.

**50**

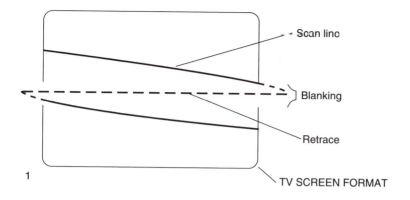

- Scan line

} Blanking

Retrace

1

TV SCREEN FORMAT

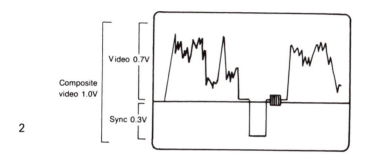

Video 0.7V

Composite
video 1.0V

Sync 0.3V

2

1. Blanking and retrace.

2. Components of composite video.

**51**

*The picture and sync must be combined.*

# Analog Sync Generator Signals (2)

### Combining Sync with Video

Take a moment and think about how the video system has been described here. The CCDs in the cameras are converting the light images into electrical signals, but the drive, blanking, and sync pulses that tell those CCDs to scan a line, turn down, retrace, turn back up, scan another line, start a new field, and so on are coming from outside the camera. Yet coming out of the camera, the video and sync information are combined. This is called *composite video*; video information without the sync information is called *noncomposite video*. So when you look at the waveform monitor, you're looking at composite video.

In a broadcast-quality system, video is always 1.0 V (140 IRE units) peak to peak (from the bottom of the sync pulse to the top of the white peaks) across a 75-$\Omega$ impedance. By looking at the figure to the right, you can see that the video portion is 0.7 V and the sync portion is 0.3 V (these figures are rounded off; the video portion is actually 0.714 V, and the sync is 0.286 V), adding up to 1.0 V. The entire video signal is less powerful than the energy from a flashlight battery.

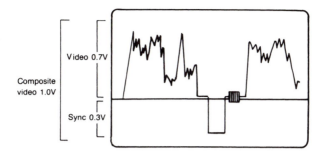

**Components of composite video.**

*The vectorscope enables you to monitor the color signals.*

# Vectorscopes

While the waveform monitor presents a graphic display of the black and white information in a picture (its luminance), a vectorscope presents a graphic display of the color information in a picture (its chrominance).

### Reading the Vectorscope
Production people must know the basics of reading and operating the *vectorscope*. Like the waveform display, a vectorscope displays signal patterns for scan lines on a CRT. Both the waveform monitor and the vectorscope continuously display 525 lines (one video frame) 30 times every second.

The vector display is round, with both black and white located in the center. The little loop in the signal to the left of center (at the 9 o'clock position) is the color burst. The primary and complementary colors are assigned locations in relation to the color burst. Going in a clockwise direction, yellow is about 10° beyond the color burst, red 76° beyond the color burst, magenta 120° beyond the color burst, blue 190° beyond the color burst, cyan 256° beyond the color burst, and green 300° beyond the color burst. This assignment of information in relation to the color burst determines the color's hue. In the figure at the top you see the typical vector display.

### Color Bar Display
*Color bars* are reference signals produced by the sync generator and placed at the beginning of a tape when it is recorded. If we read the color bar display on the vectorscope, we can adjust the video system for proper color. Probably the only time production personnel will need to use a vectorscope is for adjusting color.

The sequence of colors in the color bar display is identical to the path of the signal displayed on the vectorscope: from center (both white and black) to yellow, cyan, green, magenta, red, blue, and back to center.

Look at the vectorscope diagram. You will notice that each color falls into its own little box on the vectorscope. This indicates that you are seeing the full level of chroma. Take the red bar, for example. If the chroma were cut in half, the trace on the vectorscope for the red color would stop about halfway between the center of the display and the red box. The basic color would still be red, but it would be a paler red.

When playing back a videotape, you'll look first at the display of the color bars and, if necessary, make a few adjustments to get the same pattern as in the first figure. Once the color bars are right, the colors in the video images that follow on the tape should accurately represent the colors in the scene that was originally photographed.

**54**

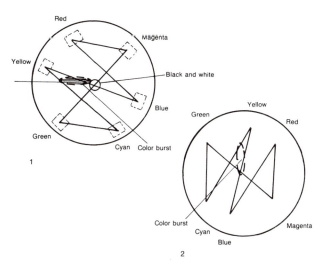

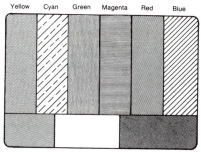

1. Schematic of a vectorscope monitor.

2. Vector display rotated 90 degrees.

3. Color bars.

*Some countries use a different system.*

# PAL

The system you have been studying up to now is called the *NTSC system*. It was named for the National Television Systems Committee, which created it in 1953 when the United States adopted its color television system. NTSC is used in North America, Japan, and many other parts of the world.

When the countries of Europe decided to adopt a color TV system, however, NTSC was 10 to 15 years old, and its weaknesses and problems were well known. In addition, technology had made long strides that allowed the Europeans to develop television systems that were superior to NTSC. The most commonly used system besides NTSC was developed in Germany and is called *PAL* for Phase Alternate Lines. The luminance and color detail of the NTSC system are not really very good. The PAL system improved luminance detail by increasing the signal bandwidth and the number of horizontal scanning lines to 625. The bandwidth is the frequency space that is needed to send a signal through the air or a cable. The wider the bandwidth, the more information can be sent. The frame rate for PAL, however, was dropped to 50 fields and 25 frames per second to match Europe's electrical frequency of 50 Hz. The waveform monitor for PAL looks the same as the NTSC waveform display. However, PAL systems set up the pedestal (in Europe they call it setup, not pedestal) at 0 instead of 7.5 as used in NTSC. This gives PAL better contrast and deeper blacks.

Except for some minor details, the color signal principles for PAL are the same as those for NTSC. One problem associated with NTSC, however, is that recording and signal transmission can induce errors in the relationship between the color burst and the color information. The PAL process averages out and cancels those errors. In PAL, the phase of the color signal is reversed by 180° from line to line (thus Phase Alternate Lines). As a result, PAL television sets always reproduce the correct hue and do not have tint or hue controls, as NTSC television sets commonly have.

PAL systems are used predominately in continental Europe, Russia, the United Kingdom, China, Australia, and some African countries. A 30-frame, 525-line version of PAL, called *PAL-M*, is used in Brazil.

The PAL and NTSC vectorscope displays look very similar. Since each line of video in the PAL system uses a color burst that is out of phase with the color burst displayed on the previous line, the vectorscope has to display both. That is the only obvious difference in the PAL vector display.

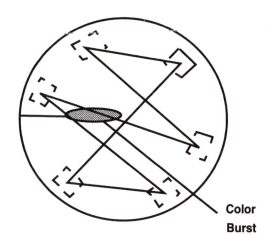

Color
Burst

**NTSC
Vectorscope
Display**

1

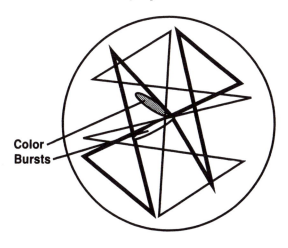

Color
Bursts

**PAL
Vectorscope
Display**

2

1. NTSC vectorscope display.

2. PAL vectorscope display.

# Analog Sync Flow Diagrams

Where do the various sync, drive, and blanking pulses go? The easiest way to illustrate the paths of these components is by using *flow diagrams*. Flow diagrams are very handy things to be able to read. They use geometric shapes to represent various pieces of equipment, and lines to represent the wires that connect the equipment. Flow diagrams enable you to see how the various components of a video system are integrated electronically. Most studios are designed using flow diagrams since, if something needs to be changed, it's much easier to erase something on a diagram and draw a new line before a studio is built than it is to rip out a wall to add a new cable after the studio has been finished.

Take a look at the sync flow diagram. This diagram is an electrical map of a typical studio video system. It charts the electrical pulses going into the cameras, as opposed to the camera flow diagrams (discussed later) that trace the electrical flow leaving the cameras. On the left-hand side of the diagram is a box labeled Sync Generator. On the left side of the box is an output labeled Black (reference or black burst). Rather than having separate outputs for each of the drives blanking, and sync pulse we use *black burst*, sometimes just called the reference signal. Black burst is analogous to a composite video signal but instead of having a picture it has black. Thus, it carries all of the necessary sync signals with it. This is what the other equipment in the studio lock up to.

## Distribution Amplifiers

Follow the path of the reference signal. You'll see that the path goes to the right and comes to a triangle that is labeled DA 1. That stands for distribution amplifier. A distribution amplifier is a piece of equipment that takes an input signal and gives you multiple output signals of that same input signal. So if we have a reference signal coming into the pulse DA, our diagram shows that we have six of the same reference signals coming out of it. This is very handy since, unlike home video and stereo, you can't use splitters and other such items because they degrade the signal too much. As its name implies, the distribution amplifier avoids this problem partly by amplifying the multiple outputs it produces. The first output goes to camera 1, and the second goes to camera 2.

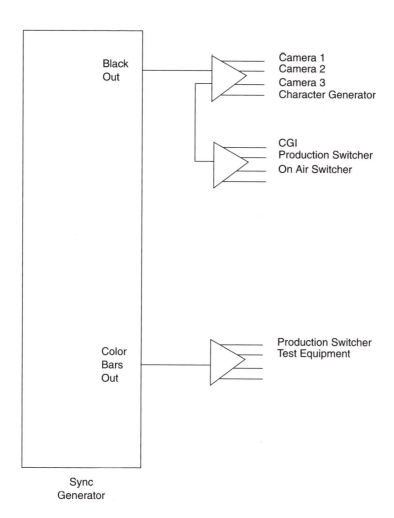

Black
Out

Camera 1
Camera 2
Camera 3
Character Generator

CGI
Production Switcher
On Air Switcher

Color
Bars
Out

Production Switcher
Test Equipment

Sync
Generator

# Camera Flow Diagrams

Take a look now at the flow diagrams for the cameras. As previously mentioned, this diagram traces output from the cameras to their ultimate destinations. The camera head is labeled Studio Camera 1, and its output goes to its CCU (camera control unit). The CCU has outputs labeled Video Out, R (red), G (green), and B (blue). The Video Out output is a fully encoded color output and goes from the CCU to a video distribution amplifier (VDA). The first VDA output goes to the main monitor wall. This is the monitor that the director looks at to decide what picture to put on the air. The second VDA output goes to the video control area. This allows the engineer to look at the various video sources to check for problems and fix them before they get too serious. The third VDA output goes to the production switcher. This allows the technical director to "punch up" the picture that the director has selected. The final VDA output goes to the patch panel. Patch panels are like switchboards; they tie all of the system components together.

The RGB outputs are the individual color components of the picture and may be kept separate throughout the studio that is set up for component operation (to be discussed later). The component outputs may also be routed to certain special effects units such as a chroma keyer.

Dropping down to camera 2, you see that it is just the same as camera 1. If there were additional cameras in the system, camera 3, 4, . . . would be the same as 2. Whether you're in a small 2-camera studio at a school or are using 48 cameras at the Super Bowl, they would all be set up in a similar manner.

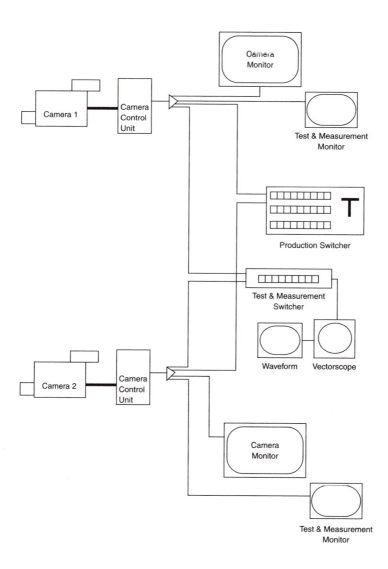

Camera 1

Camera Control Unit

Camera Monitor

Test & Measurement Monitor

Production Switcher

Test & Measurement Switcher

Waveform    Vectorscope

Camera 2

Camera Control Unit

Camera Monitor

Test & Measurement Monitor

# Combining Sync and Camera Flow Diagrams

You can combine aspects of the two flow diagrams by eliminating a few parts and combining others to make it simpler. Follow the route of the reference signal. Following the reference signal in the figure at the right, you see that it goes from the sync generator to a DA. The first DA output goes directly to the production switcher. The second DA output goes to the camera 1 CCU. From the CCU, it goes to the camera head and is combined with the video information. That composite video leaves the camera head, returns to the CCU, and from there goes to the switcher. The third DA output follows a similar path: DA to CCU, to camera head, back to CCU, and to the switcher.

Although only one specific system has been discussed, all systems are basically alike, whether using 2 cameras or 20. There will be differences, but the basic technique of running the sync through DAs to the various cameras and taking the composite video from the cameras through DAs to their various destinations will be similar in any professional situation.

**Out-of-Phase Cameras**
If you study the figure for a moment, you'll see that each of the paths is a different length. Since electricity travels at a constant speed, it will take the sync signals different amounts of time to follow each of the paths. Thus, sync on each path will arrive at the switcher at different times and the cameras will be *out of phase*. What happens if you're on camera 1 and you want to fade it down while you're fading up camera 2 (this is called a dissolve)? Which color burst, for example, will the switcher lock up to? It can only use one at a time.

The switcher will lock up on the color burst from camera 1, but as the dissolve progresses, the colors on camera 2 will look funny since they're referenced to the color burst of camera 1 instead of their own. When the dissolve is completed and camera 2 is fully "up," the switcher will lock to the color burst of camera 2 and the colors will snap back to normal. Fortunately, circuits in the cameras can be adjusted to compensate for the difference in distances traveled by the color bursts. However, if the cameras are not set properly and are out of phase, the problem described above will result.

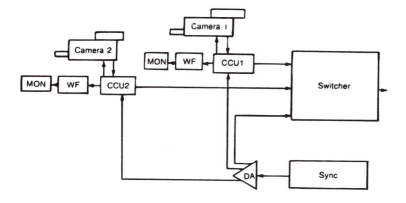

**Combining sync and camera flow.**

*Switchers allow you to choose among video sources.*

# Video Switchers

The *video switcher* is the keystone around which the rest of the TV studio is built. The *switcher* is a piece of equipment that allows you to choose from many incoming video sources and make transitions or other special effects between those sources. The sophistication of a switcher determines what transitions can be used between shots, what kind of special effects can be used, and how frequently they can be used. The capabilities of various switchers run from the very simple to the mind-boggling, and their prices follow suit.

### Vertical Interval Switchers
The standard type of switcher is the *vertical interval switcher*. This switcher has special circuitry that delays any cuts until the entire system is in vertical blanking — the vertical interval. Since vertical blanking happens 60 times a second, the delay is very small — imperceptible to humans — but it ensures sharp, clean cuts every time. Anything that is going to be switched for use on the air must go through a vertical interval switcher.

### Component Switchers
The next type of switcher is the *component switcher*. Rather than using the complete encoded color signal, this switcher deals with the individual red, green, and blue components separately. It's almost like having three separate switchers combined into one package. The three color components travel through the switcher in parallel. This generally produces a much sharper picture and crisper special effects.

### Digital Switchers
As the video industry moves to digital video, we also need switchers that are digital. Rather than processing an analog stream of changing voltages, the *digital switcher* processes a stream of digital information. Just as with analog switchers, some digital switchers are designed to handle a single composite digital signal while others will handle separate component digital signals.

### Special Effects
Virtually all production switchers today come with special-effects capabilities. How many of those special effects there are, what they are, how well they work, and how they can be used in sequences all affect the price of the switcher. The most common switcher-effects capabilities will be discussed later.

1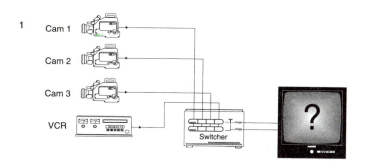

2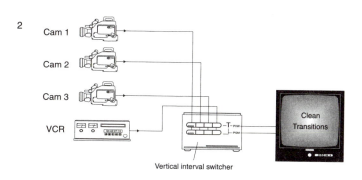

Vertical interval switcher

3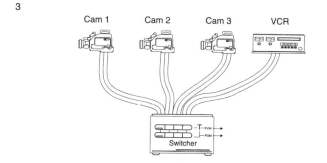

1. **Video system using a switcher.**

2. **Vertical interval switcher.**

3. **Component switcher.**

*Different uses need different switchers.*

# Switcher Applications

A switcher will be used in three common situations. In each of these applications you may find either an analog or a digital switcher. In a new facility, you are most likely going to find digital equipment. Older facilities are converting to digital, but that is where you are most likely to find analog equipment.

### Production and Editing Switchers

The first of these situations is in production. Production here refers to creating finished video that will ultimately be seen by a viewing audience: news, commercials, dramas, comedies, instruction, and just about anything else you can think of. These productions may require anything from the simplest to the most complex production switchers to accomplish the desired results.

### On-Air Switchers

The *on-air switcher* generally coordinates sources of finished production and sends output directly to the transmitter. It will be switching between various videotape machines, network feeds, satellite feeds, and the studio. These switchers are almost always *audio-follows-video switchers*. That means that when the technical director pushes a button on the switcher, it changes both the picture and the sound. That's not the case with production switchers, where any changes in sound must be done separately. Since anything that normally goes to the transmitter has the picture and sound together, this makes things much quicker and easier for the technical director. On-air switchers usually have limited special-effects capabilities. Because anything going to the transmitter is usually a finished product, there's little need for special effects at this stage.

### Routing Switchers

The final switcher application is for routing. Say that you're working in a large school system and you need to send seven or eight programs to different classrooms at the same time. You would use a *routing switcher* to accomplish this task. Routing switchers are often audio-follows-video units, and they're frequently very large. Some of the newer models use advanced electronics that permit far greater flexibility using much less space.

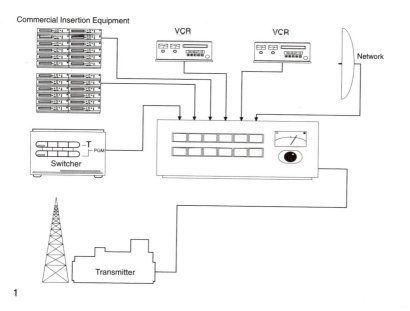

Commercial Insertion Equipment

VCR  VCR  Network

Switcher

Transmitter

1

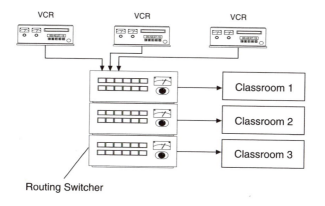

VCR  VCR  VCR

Classroom 1

Classroom 2

Classroom 3

Routing Switcher

2

1. **On-air switcher.**

2. **Routing switcher.**

*The switcher is the heart of the studio.*

# Production Switcher Flow Diagram

Take a look at the flow diagram of a switcher integrated into a simple video system. This switcher is very basic, and a lot has been left out to keep things as simple as possible. As you can see, this system has four cameras. Now follow the outputs of each camera. In each case, the output goes to a distribution amplifier and from there one output goes to a monitor and another goes to the production switcher.

### Switcher Buses

You'll notice that at the switcher there are two rows of buttons, each row a duplicate of the other. These rows of buttons are called *buses*. They're what give you the ability to cut and dissolve between cameras.

### Switcher Outputs

The switcher has two outputs. The preview (PVW) output allows the director to see the next shot before it is used. The program (PGM) output is what is intended to be recorded or transmitted. In this example, the final output is both recorded and transmitted.

The preview output is going to a preview monitor for the director's use. The program output is going to a distribution amplifier, and from there one output goes to the program monitor and another one goes to the on-air switcher, where it is fed to the transmitter. The other two program DA outputs are going to videotape recorders (VTRs) where the show is recorded.

Production switchers will usually have a master program bus (PGM). Whatever is punched up on this row of buttons will be the picture being recorded and sent out to the viewers. Below the program bus will be a preview (PVW) or preset (PST) bus. Next to these two rows of buttons will be a "Take" button and a T-shaped handle. Whatever the director wants to see next will be "punched up" on the PVW/PST bus. Pushing the "Take" button will create a cut from what was on the PGM bus to what is on the PVW/PST bus. Moving the T-shaped handle will create a dissolve between the two video sources. In either case the sources on the PVW/PST bus will swap positions or flip-flop with the source on the PGM bus.

This is a simplified diagram of a very basic system, but if you study it, you'll get a good idea of how the basic components are integrated.

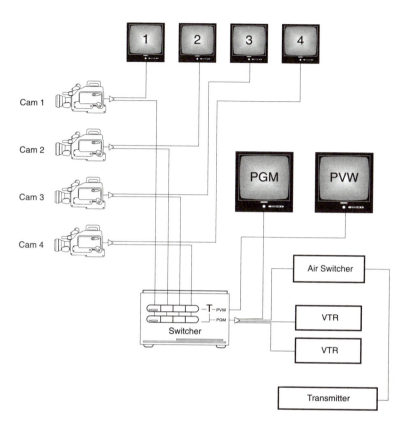

**Switcher flow diagram.**

# Switcher Transitions and Special Effects

All production switchers are capable of at least three transitions: cuts, fades, and dissolves. *Cuts* are instantaneous changes from one picture to another. A *fade-in* is a transition that starts with a blank screen (black) that grows progressively brighter until the full picture appears at its normal intensity. A *fade-out* is the opposite, beginning with a full picture that decreases in intensity to a blank screen. A *dissolve* is much like a fade, except that as one picture is fading out, another is fading in, so there is always a picture on the screen. Cuts, fades, and dissolves represent the meat and potatoes of television; they make up most of the transitions used in dramas and comedies. All the other fancy effects that a switcher can produce are often called the "bells and whistles." They're there for flash, sparkle, and pizzazz. If your content is solid, you don't need many bells and whistles, although the American public has come to accept them as part of the package. This is not to say that these special effects are valueless. Some can, and often do, add to the content of the program.

## Wipes

*Wipes* are transitions between video sources that are marked by visible edges (sometimes the edge is diffused). Rather than one picture fading out as the other fades in as with a dissolve, in a wipe the new picture replaces the old one by means of a geometric form moving through the old picture. It might be a horizontal or vertical line moving across the picture, or it might be a star or circle coming from the center and expanding until it takes over the whole picture. The number of wipe patterns available seems unlimited. Some switchers come with 40 standard wipe patterns, with still others available as options. Wipes that aren't completed, thus leaving parts of two pictures visible, are called *split screens*.

1

2

3

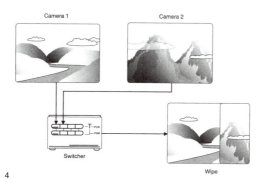

4

1. Fade-in.

2. Fade-out.

3. Dissolve.

4. Wipe.

*Keys are "holes" that need to be filled.*

# Special Effects Keys — Luminance Keys

Keys are among the most common and useful special effects. *Keys* are essentially holes cut into a video picture that are filled with material from another source. Different types of keys rely on different information to determine the shape and nature of the holes and how they are filled. *Luminance keys* are triggered by differences in brightness (contrast). The hole in the original video is cut according to contrast differences supplied by a programmed source. The pattern the system derives from this source is called the *key source* or *key signal*. The figure at the right shows a common use of luminance keys.

Camera 2 is providing the key source — the bright star against the black background. The switcher receives the signal from camera 2 and reads the star as a pattern, the key source, based on the difference in brightness between the star and the background. The system cuts a hole in the shape of a star in the camera 1 video.

The hole can be filled in one of several ways. If the pattern that cuts the hole also fills the hole, it is a *self-fill key*. If the hole is filled by artificially created color from within the switcher itself, it is called a *matte key*. The hole can also be filled with a third source — video from a third camera, for example.

The greater the key source contrast between the desired pattern and its background, the more easily the key operates. White on black is ideal, but for key sources that don't have as much contrast, there will always be a "clip" adjustment that will allow you to compensate. Keys don't have to be geometric patterns. They can be (and often are) white lettering on a black background — titles, for instance. You certainly can key in other shapes, such as a white horse running against a dark background.

### Linear or Transparent Keys

The type of key we have been discussing where the key is punched completely through the video is also called a *nonlinear key*. A *linear* or *transparent key* allows you to lay a key over the video without punching all of the way through it. This will allow the audience to see through the key to what is going on behind it. This is especially useful for sporting events where a nonlinear key could block the action caused by a sudden change on the field.

The most common use of the luminance key is for adding titles to video — for example, the names of the announcers which appear in the bottom third of the screen.

Camera 1

Program

Camera 2

**Luminance key.**

**73**

*Chroma keys use a special color to cut a video hole.*

# Special Effects Keys — Chroma Keys

*Chroma keys* also cut a hole out of the video, but unlike luminance keys, the triggering device is not contrast. It's a particular color in the subject video (the video receiving the special effect). In a chroma key, the system detects the chosen color in the subject video and wherever it sees that color replaces it with information from another video source. In the first figure the person (or talent) is in front of a chroma key window. The camera that shoots the chroma key window is called the *source camera*. Any other video source can supply the fill video, but in this example camera 2 has been used. Where the system sees the selected color (the window), it replaces that information with the corresponding information from the fill camera. Thus, you get a rocket launch in the studio. If you were to make the entire background the chroma key window, then that background would be filled. The second figure illustrates this. You now see the entire area behind the talent filled with the launch because the entire background has become the key window. The chroma key circuitry will try to fill in the source anywhere it sees the chosen color. It is for this reason that primary colors are used for the key window. If you chose yellow for your key window, for example, the system would not only lock up to yellow, but it would try to lock up to anything containing yellow's components, red and green. Thus, the chroma key would try to lock up to almost everything but the color blue.

Since people almost always appear in the chroma key source picture, red is not used for the key window very often. After all, there is quite a bit of red in the flesh tones of people. Blue and green are the colors most commonly used for chroma key windows. Thus, the industry terms are blue screen and green screen.

Anyone wearing clothing that is the same color as the chroma key window will present problems, since the clothing might be keyed out as well. Since white includes all colors of light, the chroma keyer may try to lock up to it, but this will usually appear as an incomplete key. Although black is the lack of colors, it too can create problems. Small patches of black, particularly shadows, may also be keyed over. When the system is scanning and it comes to a void of color (black), it may not be sure what to do, so it keys over the area. Larger areas of black may not cause a problem because they're large enough for the system to determine exactly what they are.

The chroma key also has a clip control. In addition, there is a hue (chroma) control that allows you to choose the color to be keyed out, and there is a gain control that controls the strength of the source picture.

**74**

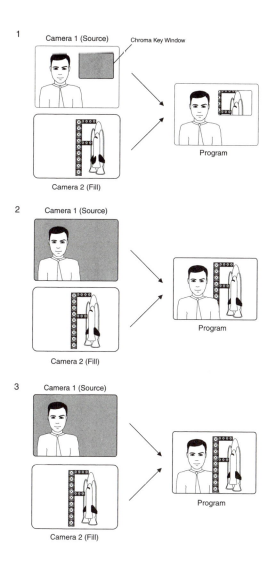

1. Small chroma key window.

2. Full background chroma key window.

3. Talent wearing coat same color as key window.

*A studio usually has one of several video signal systems.*

# Composite versus Component Video

### Problems of Composite Video
You learned that encoding is the process of combining the three chrominance channels and the luminance channel into a single composite video signal. Many pieces of video equipment need to decode this composite signal into its component parts in order to process and use it. Of course, the component signals must then be re-encoded before the composite signal can be sent on its way from that piece of equipment. Every time the signal is encoded or decoded, it is distorted a little and some noise is added. As creative people want to use more sophisticated production techniques and consumers want a better picture, demands are being made for better quality video. There are a number of approaches to the problem.

### Component Video
Taking the separate RGB outputs from each camera and running them directly to the switcher bypasses the entire encoding circuitry of the camera. This provides a cleaner, sharper picture. Keys come across especially well with this system. Of course, to get the most out of this system the entire studio needs to be component oriented — cameras, distribution amplifiers, switchers, and character generators. Upgrading a system to component requires reengineering the entire control room, since three cables will now have to be installed for every one that was there before.

Most equipment that originates video, such as cameras and character generators, is easily integrated into a component system. This equipment already generates RGB signals, so it doesn't take much to bypass the encoder. The DAs and switchers, however, are much more expensive. As a result, it is going to take a big budget to convert the entire studio to component video.

### Y/C
A less expensive component system that produces higher quality video than composite video is *Y/C*. In technical terms, Y stands for the luminance information and C stands for the chrominance information. Using a Y/C (sometimes called S) system eliminates much of the encoding and decoding problems inherent in composite video.

To get an idea of how this system works, take a look at Y/C VTRs. Rather than laying down an entire field of composite video in one track, a Y/C must lay down the Y and C information separately to make a field. This provides much better quality at a reasonable cost.

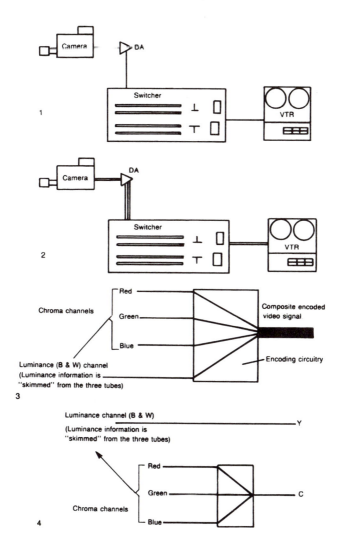

1. Composite system.

2. Component system.

3. Composite video.

4. Y/C video.

# Color Difference Component Video

If you are in a studio setting where you can use individual cables for each of the red, green, and blue channels, you don't have to worry very much about how much bandwidth they use. If, however, you have to send a color signal through the air or several video signals through one cable, bandwidth can become a problem. To save bandwidth, engineers developed *color difference component video*. This system still uses three different signals to carry the complete picture, but the engineers came up with a method that eliminates the redundancy found in the RGB channels. First is the Y channel, which is all of the luminance channel. We learned earlier that the green channel makes up 59% of the total color signal, so most of the luminance information comes from the green channel. But the red and blue channels also have luminance information. Since we already have that in the Y channel, we don't need the parts of it that are in the red and blue channels. So it is subtracted from those two channels, leaving red minus luminance (R-Y) and blue minus luminance (B-Y). This gives us pure red information and pure blue information and luminance information. When the picture is reassembled, the necessary luminance information is taken from the Y channel and added to blue and red. Anything left in the Y channel has to be for the green channel, and the picture is thus reconstructed. Using the Y (R-Y) (B-Y) color difference system saves a tremendous amount of bandwidth while keeping all of the advantages of high-quality component video.

The Y/C, RGB, and color difference systems are all different types of component video. Most systems that are set up for RGB can also use the color difference system.

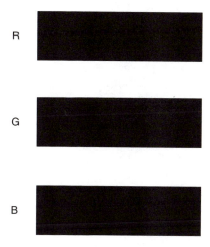

Bandwidth requirements of RGB component video.

Bandwidth requirements of color difference component video.

# Digital Special Effects

Wipes, split screens, luminance, and chroma keys make up the majority of special effects on the typical production switcher. There is another group of special effects called *digital video effects (DVE)*. Digital technology will be discussed in greater detail later, but it is appropriate to describe some basic digital effects here. Most production switchers made today have digital video effects as a standard feature. Most DVE units have the following effects.

### Compressions

*Compressions* are effects that change the entire aspect of the picture: the picture is made longer, or higher, or the entire picture is compressed into a smaller area. A common use of this technique is called *chroma key tracking*. With this effect the entire fill video is compressed to fit into the chroma key window. In the first figure, the entire launch has been compressed to fit into the smaller chroma key window. Many stations avoid the chroma key process entirely by compressing what would be the fill video and inserting it into a predetermined space in the program video.

### Pushes

Another common digital effect is a *push*. A push, as you might expect, is where one video source pushes another off the screen.

### Flips

There are several types of *flips*. In a page flip, the picture rotates around one edge of the screen as if you were turning the page of a book. Other flips can rotate around a central vertical or horizontal axis.

### Rotations

*Rotating cubes and spheres* are two other digital effects, with video images making up the outer surfaces of these geometric shapes.

### Other Special Effects

The array of possible digital effects is virtually limitless. Video images can be twisted, distorted, curled, and exploded into fragments and miraculously reassembled. In most situations, the effects are almost infinitesimal.

Many digital effects have become practical and affordable through the development of programmable digital switchers. These switchers can hold in their memories a sequence or combination of special effects and then recall the arrangement on a command from the user.

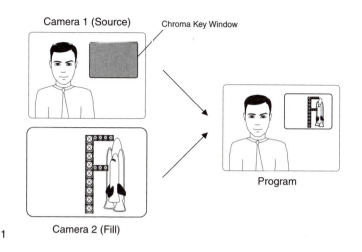

Camera 1 (Source)

Chroma Key Window

Camera 2 (Fill)

Program

1

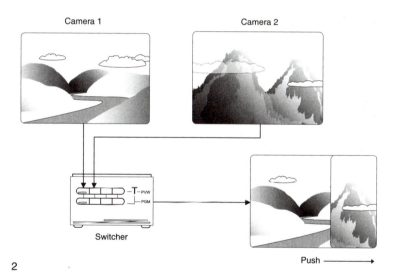

Camera 1

Camera 2

Switcher

Push ⟶

2

1. **Chroma key tracking.**

2. **Pushes.**

*A computer is needed to figure out some effects.*

# Digital Interpolation

Digital video is really a series of numbers that represent the brightness and color information for each pixel on the TV screen. Digital video effects are made possible by manipulating those numbers or by creating new numbers through a mathematical process called *interpolation*.

## Manipulation

Let's assume that you wanted to compress video into a smaller space such as is described on the previous page in the chroma key tracking example. You want to take the same information and push it into a smaller space, but the number of pixels on the screen is fixed and cannot be changed. You have to remove some information to fit the available space. Assume that you have one line of video that you want to compress down to a space of a half line. A line of video has about 700 pixels. In the digital stream, the brightness of each pixel will be represented by a number between 0 and 255. So in the digital world, a line of video would be a stream of 700 numbers. If we removed every other number in the line, we would be left with a value for 350 pixels or a half line of video. The one line of video has been compressed to a half line.

## Interpolation

But what if you wanted to take a small part of the picture and expand it to fill the screen? Let's reverse the preceding example. We want to start with a half line of video (350 pixels) and expand it to a full line (700 pixels). Let's deal with only the digital values for the first 8 pixels of that line. We'll say the digital values for those first eight pixels are 0, 20, 40, 60, 80, 100, 120, and 140. If we want to double the length of the line, we have to expand this information and put an additional pixel between each of the values above: 0, ?, 20, ?, 40, ?, 60, ?, 80, ?, 100, ?, 120, ?, 140. But what value do we give to each of these new pixels? In this example, it is pretty easy to figure out because the brightness of the picture is increasing at a steady rate. There is a difference of 20 for each of the values we have. By taking half of that, we know how much to add to the value of each pixel and we get this result: 0, 10, 20, 30, 40, 50, 60, 70, 80, 90, 100, 110, 120, 130, 140. We have expanded a line of video, and the new line is consistent with the part of the old line with which we started. This process is called *interpolation*. Of course, in reality, a computer is actually doing this for you. This type of manipulation takes very fast computer processing speeds.

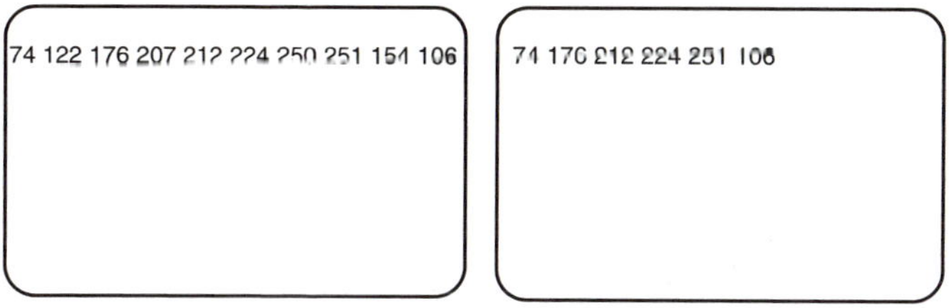

| 74 122 176 207 212 224 250 251 154 106 | 74 176 212 224 251 106 |

1

| 20 40 60 80 100 | 20 30 40 50 60 70 80 90 100 120 |

2

1. A video line compressed to half a video line.

2. A half of a video line expanded to a full line using interpolation.

Digital Interpolation

# Analog Videotape Recording Technology

### Recorders

Videotape recording enables the practical recording and immediate or future playback of a high-quality video image. Video recording imprints magnetic signal patterns onto a specially prepared tape. Two of the key aspects of this process are the tape itself and the recording head.

### Videotape

The foundation of videotape is a strong plastic ribbon. On the back of the tape is a slick surface that helps the tape move through a mechanical transport smoothly. On the front side of the tape are metal oxides mixed with a binding compound that secures the oxides to the tape. If you pass a magnet close to these oxides, they will be left with their own, much weaker, magnetic field. The stronger the magnet that arranges these oxide particles, the stronger the induced magnetic field.

### Recording Heads

In order to record the desired information, a special electromagnet called a *recording head* has to be used. For video, the head is very small, made of very thin metal (about the thickness of a fingernail). The head is hollow, like a tube. Thin wire coiled around the other side of the head connects the head to the rest of the recorder.

In the second figure at the right, the head has been enlarged many, many times. Although the figure shows the head by itself, in reality it would be mounted in a small nonmetallic enclosure. The head and enclosure are often shaped something like a piece of bread. The curved surface is the one through which electrical information is exchanged with tape. As the changing analog voltage (the composite video signal) from the camera electronics is processed and flows through the head, it causes corresponding changes in the electromagnetic field that the video recording head produces. This leaves varied magnetic fields in the oxides on the tape. This is the basic recording process.

The playback process is just the reverse. The magnetically encoded tape is passed across a video head that has no signal flowing through it. The magnetic field on the tape induces a signal into the head corresponding to the varied magnetic fields on the tape. Thus, you reproduce the same analog signal from the tape that was induced onto the tape from the camera source.

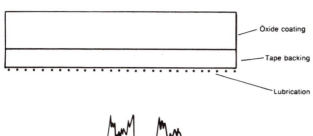

1

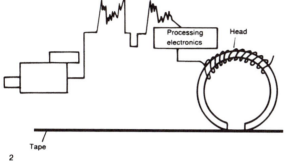

Tape

2

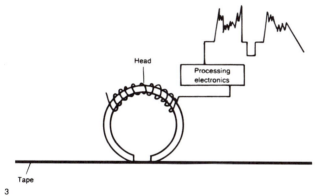

Tape

3

1. Cross-section of magnetic tape.

2. Recording on tape.

3. Videotape playback.

# Analog Video Recording Standards and Formats

### Audio versus Video Recording

The recording process is essentially the same for both audio and video recording, but about 200 times more information can be found in the video signal than in an audio signal. You can fit only so much information onto a given piece of tape. As a result, there's simply not enough room for all the video information using audio recording technology.

The biggest difference is that audio heads are stationary. Video uses several smaller heads mounted on a rotating disc. This allows more information to be put down in the same space.

### Helical Video Recording

Helical tape machines are the standard of the broadcast industry. At least a half dozen different formats of helical videotape machines might be found in professional broadcast operations. Although none will interchange with the others, they all have some things in common. Whereas the number of heads mounted on the headwheel will vary with different formats, all helical headwheels are mounted at an angle and rotate in almost the opposite direction to the tape. The magnetic heads lay down long slanting video tracks on the tape. Each of these tracks contains one field of video information: video lines, blanking, and sync information. Therefore, if you were to slow down or stop the tape with the headwheel spinning, you would still get 60 fields of information a second, so slow motion and freeze frames are possible with helical machines. However, because of some other problems that will be discussed later, these are not broadcast-quality slow motion or freeze frames.

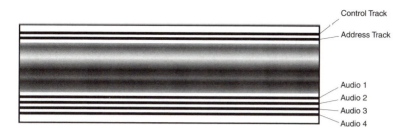

Control Track
Address Track
Audio 1
Audio 2
Audio 3
Audio 4

**Helical videotape.**

# Other Tracks and Lockup (1)

## Sound and Control Tracks

So far only the video information recorded on tape has been discussed, but there is a lot of other information needed on the tape. Sound, for example, also has to be recorded. All of the nonvideo information is recorded using stationary heads much like the heads used in standard audiotape recorders. The number, type, and placement of these other tracks will vary with the specific format of the machine being used.

One of the most important of these other tracks, and one that is common to all formats, is the *control track*. During the recording process, the vertical sync pulses are recorded on the control track. The control track thus helps stabilize the tape's playback speed. You know that the vertical sync pulses are laid down at a rate of 60 pulses a second (one for each field). The regularity of these pulses makes the control track important for other reasons that will be discussed next.

## VTR Lockup

The more precise we can make the VTR's playback speed, the more accurate the playback will be to the recording. When the machine gets up to full speed and everything is as stable as it is going to get, we say the machine is "locked up." There are several degrees of lockup, and each additional step adds a little more stability.

## Capstan Lock

The first degree of lockup is called *capstan lock*, suitable mainly for home videotape recorders. Capstan lock is not a very stable state. The machine essentially relies on the stability of the power source for a constant base. If the power coming out of the wall varies, so does your tape speed because the speed control circuitry is very simple.

Control Track

Address Track

Audio 1
Audio 2
Audio 3
Audio 4

**Helical videotape.**

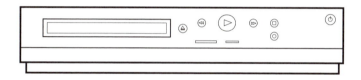

**Capstan lock machines have no special speed control circuitry.**

# Other Tracks and Lockup (2)

### Vertical Lock (Capstan Servo)

The next level is called *vertical lock* or *capstan servo*. This is the minimum degree of lockup for professional production. Capstan servo machines make use of the control track (remember it?) and incoming sync from the sync generator. If you recall, vertical sync pulses are laid down on the control track, and, since they come from the sync generator, they are laid down at very precise intervals. A capstan servo machine is also hooked up to the sync generator and has a special circuit to compare the number of incoming vertical sync pulses from the sync generator with the number of pulses being played back from the control track. Since both pulses ultimately originate from the same source, there should be the same number of pulses in the same amount of time. The vertical sync pulses that come from the sync generator act as a clock. If there are 60 pulses from the sync generator and only 55 from the control track, then the tape is moving too slowly and the capstan servo is signaled to increase the playback speed. But if there are 60 pulses from the sync generator and 63 from the control track, then the tape is moving too fast and the capstan servo is signaled to slow it down.

The big advantage of vertical lock is that a vertical interval switcher will be able to switch to tape from anything without a breakup.

### Frame Lock

The next level of lockup is called *frame lock* and follows the same rule of comparing information from the sync generator with playback information to help regulate tape playback speed. There was no attempt in vertical lock to match an even field pulse with an even field pulse or an odd field pulse with an odd field pulse. That's what the frame lock circuitry does. It determines whether the vertical sync pulse coming from the sync generator is for an odd or an even field. Then it speeds up or slows down the tape machine until the pulses off the control track match: odd for odd and even for even. This makes the tape playback speed just a little more precise.

### Horizontal Lock

We now have the fields matched, but each field has 262.5 lines, and each line has a horizontal sync pulse. This leads to the next level of lockup, *horizontal lock*. The horizontal lock circuitry compares the number of incoming horizontal sync pulses with the number of played-back horizontal sync pulses. The VTR headwheel then speeds up or slows down the tape in an attempt to match the two horizontal pulses.

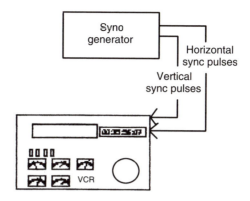

1. The horizontal lock machine tries to match every horizontal sync pulse played back to a horizontal sync pulse from the sync generator.

*The VTR cannot play back at a constant speed.*

# Time Base Error

The *tape transport system* is a very important and complex mechanism that pulls the tape across the tape heads. It is also the source of a major problem in videotape recording. The problem is that it's impossible to build such a system that operates at a truly constant speed, and that means that it is impossible for the machine to play back tape at precisely the same speed at which it was recorded. You can come pretty close, but in some cases that's not good enough.

If you review the section on sync generators, you'll see that the video signal is composed of some very precise bits of timing information. Because all this video and sync timing information is coming from the sync generator and camera, it is being recorded very accurately. But since the VTR can't play back the tape at exactly the same speed at which it was recorded, the playback information won't be as precise as what was recorded. This inability of a VTR to play back at exactly the same speed is called *time base error*. Time base error is measured in lines. It takes 63.5 $\mu$sec to scan a horizontal video line. If the playback signal is 63.5 $\mu$sec off from where it should be, there is one line of error.

Dealing with time base error can thus be an integral part of videotape recording. If the amount of error is small or can be corrected, the resulting picture problems will be minimal. However, a large error or, in some cases, any error at all can produce terrible jitters, jumps, and rolls in the picture.

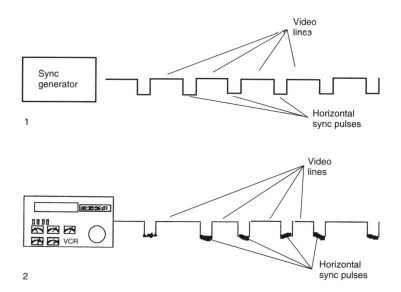

1. Sync generator puts out very stable signals with each video line being exactly the same length and the horizontal sync pulses falling at the same intervals. This precise signal is then recorded on videotape.

2. Because the videotape machine cannot play back at an absolutely precise speed, the video lines vary somewhat in length and the horizontal sync pulses are reproduced at varying intervals. The degradation of the sync pulses comes from generation drop, not from time base error.

*Field conditions can make precision playback more difficult.*

# External Causes of Time Base Error

A VTR that spends all of its time in the studio will have relatively little time base error, assuming that the equipment is in good condition and properly used. But VTRs that are used in the field have an additional chance for time base error. Time base error can result from any change in the actual composition of the tape, generally owing to variations in air temperature, humidity, recorder position, and recorder movement. When a portable machine is used in the field, it is subjected to constantly changing conditions. It might be in the bright sun one minute and in the cool shade of a tree the next. You might be shooting at the fog-shrouded seashore in the morning and in the hot, dry desert later that afternoon. Changes in temperature and humidity will cause the tape to expand and contract. How might this result in time base error? Assume that you're shooting outside on a hot, sunny day. This will cause the tape to expand. After a hot afternoon of work, you return to the nice air-conditioned studio to edit the piece. The cool temperature of the studio causes the tape to contract. But even if the VTR could play back the tape at exactly the same speed as it was recorded, there would still be a problem. Since the tape has contracted, the video tracks have also contracted, so it will take a little less time for the head to scan them. Additional time base error has been created.

### Gyroscopic Time Base Error
*Gyroscopic time base error* refers to the creation of time base problems specifically by changes in recorder position and movement. It's a very common occurrence given today's highly portable video equipment. Let's say that you've got one of those great camcorders that combine the camera and VTR in one unit. You have it up on your shoulder for some great shots, and then you swing around to follow the action. Gyroscopic time base error has been created. Gyroscopic error occurs because the spinning head drum in the VTR acts like a gyroscope. If you have ever played with a toy gyroscope or a spinning top, you know that if you try to move the toy against the plane of its rotation you will feel resistance. This is what happens inside the VTR. As the VTR is moved against the plane of rotation of the head drum, the spinning drum resists and slows down a little. When it slows down, the information will not be recorded at the proper speed. This is gyroscopic time base error. All of these factors determine how much time base error you might expect on tape playback. It could be less than a line in a studio machine, or it could add up to 20 or 30 lines (or more) on a field recorder!

**94**

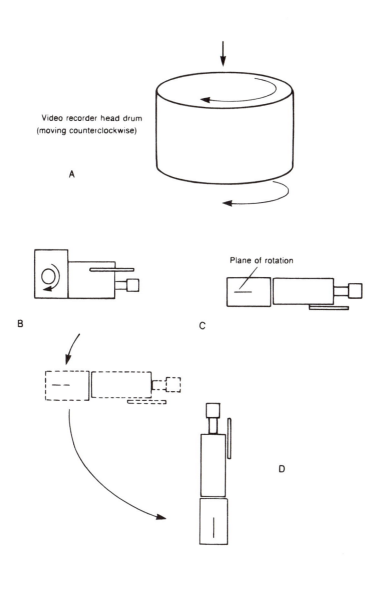

Video recorder head drum
(moving counterclockwise)

A

B

C

Plane of rotation

D

Gyroscopic time base error. (A) Forces that move against the head drum's plane of rotation will cause gyroscopic error. (B) Side view of camcorder showing head drum and rotation. (C) Top view of the same camera showing the head drum's plane of rotation. (D) Gyroscopic error is caused when the head drum's plane of rotation is changed.

*A time base corrector can fix time base error.*

# Time Base Error Correction

Time base error becomes a real problem when you try to integrate analog videotape material into a production. If you just want to play back the tape, no problem, but if you want to fade, dissolve, wipe, split screen, or key using taped material, forget it! You've got an unstable playback signal trying to match up with the very stable, sync generator controlled video system. If you try to produce any of these effects with tape, the picture will jump, jitter, roll, or tear. In short, it will look terrible. This can be corrected with a time base corrector, which can cost as much as some analog VTRs. Time base correctors will take the unstable signal coming out of the VTR and stabilize it. Exactly how they work will be discussed next.

For some analog VTRs you have to buy a separate time base corrector. Most of the better analog VTRs have time base correctors built into them. Because digital compression, to be discussed later, requires that the signal be taken apart and then reassembled before it can be fed out of the machine, most digital VTRs have a form of time base correction built into them. Many digital switchers will also have time base correction built into their input circuitry.

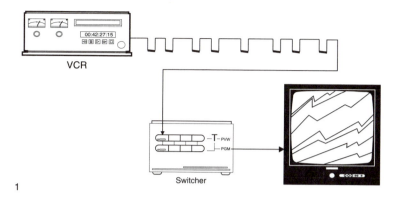

1

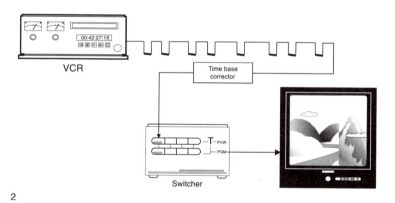

2

1. **Integrating helical VTR video without time base correction.**

2. **Integrating helical VTR video with time base correction.**

*A time base corrector turns unstable video into stable video.*

# Time Base Correctors (1)

## What a Time Base Corrector Does

Total time base error in a typical video can amount to more than 20 or 30 lines and needs to be brought down to the range of 5 to 10 nsec. A modern *time base corrector (TBC)* can do this job for us. Unstable video goes from the VTR into the TBC and stable video comes out of the TBC, which is then fed into the system.

## How a TBC Works

Of course, things are considerably more complex than this description would suggest. The biggest problem is that we need a very large memory to store the video picture in, so that it can be fed out at an even, synchronized rate. Memories that will hold a lot of analog video are very expensive and difficult to make. However, computer memories are relatively inexpensive and common, so if we could get our analog video into computer form, we could make good use of those memories. That's just what happens. As you learned earlier, however, computers can only deal with numbers. The first thing that happens after unstable video enters the time base corrector from the videotape machine is that it goes through an analog to digital (A to D) converter. From there the information goes to a large computer memory.

## Horizontal Sync as a Clock

A method needs to be devised to release this digital video information in sync with the rest of the system. As you might suspect, we go back to the sync generator, which is hooked up to the TBC. The horizontal sync pulses from the sync generator act as a clock. Each time a horizontal sync pulse reaches a special gate circuit, it lets one line of digital video information out of the memory.

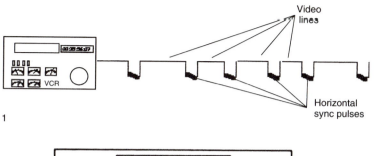

1

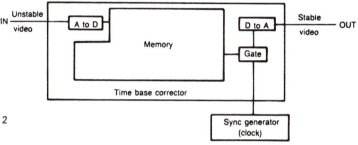

2

1. Because the videotape machine cannot play back at an absolutely precise speed, the video lines vary somewhat in length and the horizontal sync pulses fall at varying intervals.

2. Time base corrector.

*The digital information must be changed back to analog.*

# Time Base Correctors (2)

### D to A Conversion
This digital video can't be integrated with analog video, so it has to go through a D to A (digital to analog) converter to be changed back to analog information. As a result, corrected analog video comes out of the TBC.

### Video Proc Amp
In addition, TBCs have an internal *proc amp* (video processing amplifier). As previously noted, the quality of the sync itself may have deteriorated owing to factors such as copying a tape. However, proc amps have their own sync generators, so that when the distorted sync comes off the tape, the proc amp strips it away and inserts new, clean sync in its place. Proc amps also enable you to adjust some of the video parameters, such as brightness, chroma intensity, phase, and pedestal (black level).

### Window of Correction
Each TBC will have what is called a *window of correction*. As you might suspect, this tells you the maximum amount of time base error it can correct. A TBC with a four-line window might be fine for VTRs and tapes that never leave the climate-controlled confines of a studio, but it would be almost useless with tape shot out in the field. A TBC with a 32-line window will cost a good deal more money, but it should be able to handle anything shot in the studio or the field.

**100**

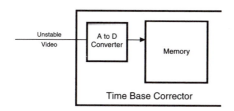

Time Base Corrector

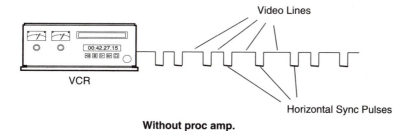

Without proc amp.

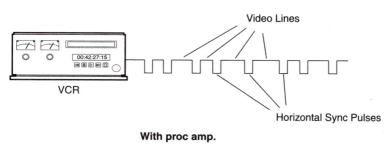

With proc amp.

# Larger Analog Sync Problems and Solutions

### Nonsynchronous Sources

TBCs are great for correcting the relatively minor errors found on tape, but some video sources are totally out of sync with the studio. For example, when the networks do a football game, do you think there's a cable going from the sync generator on the ground all the way up to the blimp that's getting those dramatic aerial shots? Of course not! Since there is no incoming sync for the blimp camera, it has to be on its own system, and it is totally out of sync with the cameras on the ground. We say that the blimp is a nonsynchronous or wild video source. Or what about the local TV station? Each station will have its own sync generator, but the video coming into the station from a network or a satellite feed will be on a different sync generator and thus be a nonsynchronous source. If the local station wants to dissolve from the network football game to a local commercial, it could lose sync and the picture will break up.

### Frame Synchronizer

The solution to problems posed by nonsynchronous sources is the *frame synchronizer*. Although the frame synchronizer operates a little differently than a TBC, you can think of it as a TBC with a larger memory. It can hold more than a frame of video information in its memory. Like a TBC, a frame synchronizer converts lines of analog video signal into digital form and stabilizes them. However, the vertical sync rather than the horizontal sync acts as the frame synchronizer gate release signal. When it gets a vertical sync pulse from the house sync generator, the frame synchronizer feeds out a field of video information. As a result, any nonsynchronous video source can be locked up to and integrated with the system you're using. Frame store synchronizers are pretty expensive, but they're a tremendous resource since they will do anything a TBC will do, plus lock up a nonsynchronous source.

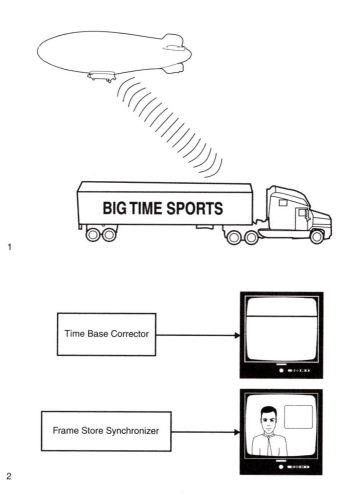

BIG TIME SPORTS

Time Base Corrector

Frame Store Synchronizer

1

2

1. Since the blimp and the remote truck are operating on separate sync generators, they are nonsynchronous.

2. A TBC feeds out one line at a time, while a frame synchronizer feeds out a field at a time.

*Slow motion and freeze frames are also possible.*

# Other Advantages of TBCs and Frame Synchronizers

### Dynamic Tracking Heads

TBCs and frame synchronizers can give you a couple of other capabilities as well. If your VTR has a dynamic tracking head, a TBC will allow you to do broadcast-quality slow motion. A *dynamic tracking head* is a video head that adjusts itself to follow the video track when the tape changes speed. When you slow down the speed of videotape playback, the relationship between the video head and the angle of the video track changes. The dynamic tracking head automatically compensates for this change and always stays centered on the video track. A TBC or frame synchronizer simply maintains the proper sync with the rest of the system, even if, as in this case, the tape speed is slowed.

### Freeze Frames

A frame store synchronizer will also let you freeze frames. When you push the freeze on a frame synchronizer, it will continuously feed out the same field of video information. Some units will also feed out a complete frame, but then you often get frame jitter. This is because the video picture is not static. In the camera, after the first field is scanned, the second interlaced field is scanned. But in the meantime, the subject of the picture may have moved just a little. So when the second field is interlaced with the first one, the subject may be offset a little, and this can cause a jitter of the subject between one field and the other.

### TBCs, VTRs, and Production

TBCs are what have made helical VTRs practical for broadcast use. TBCs and frame synchronizers have become an integral part of TV production facilities everywhere. They are the devices that started the digital revolution in video production.

Digital technology provides another advantage beyond what might be apparent from this discussion of TBCs and frame synchronizers. Unlike analog, when the digital signal is run through several pieces of equipment, there is no increase in noise. Since digital information is a series of numbers, the D to A converter will ignore any surrounding noise when it converts that number to its corresponding voltage.

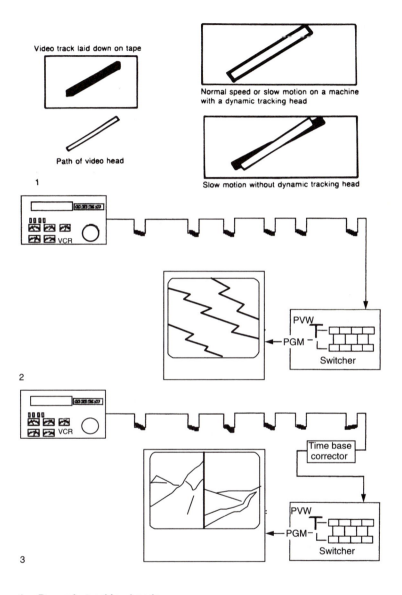

Video track laid down on tape

Path of video head

Normal speed or slow motion on a machine with a dynamic tracking head

Slow motion without dynamic tracking head

1

2

3

1. **Dynamic tracking heads.**

2. **Integrating helical VTR video without time base correction.**

3. **Integrating helical VTR video with time base correction.**

# Digital Videotape Recorders

Analog videotape has just about disappeared from the professional production scene. Digital video recording is generally of much better quality and is transparent. That means that copies are identical to the original. As long as the recording machine can tell the difference between one number and another, it will record a clean full-strength number on the tape. The first illustration on the right shows a recorder that will accept and play back only component digital signals. The same approach could also be used for composite digital video. The most commonly used digital recorders can accept and play back either analog or digital signals such as the second illustration on the right shows.

### DV Video

One of the newest and fastest growing digital video formats is *DV*. DV includes a wide range of options ranging from low-cost MiniDV, which uses cassettes smaller than audio cassettes and is available in the consumer market, to full-sized DV, which uses much larger cassettes and is designed for the professional market. Full-sized DV tape decks will play back MiniDV of the same manufacturer. DV provides high-quality recording at a modest price. It will also accept an analog input and provide an analog output. For these reasons it is found in a wide array of local stations and production companies.

The major problem with DV is the lack of uniform compatibility between manufacturers. Tapes recorded on one manufacturer's machine may not play back on machines made by another company. Therefore, when choosing DV it is important to make sure all of the machines you buy are compatible with each other.

Videotape recorders have served us well for 50 years, but their days are numbered. Even the relatively new and popular DV format is being replaced by disc-based systems (to be discussed a little later) that use the DV CODEC. Compared to other systems coming on line now, videotape is unreliable, time consuming, and requires a lot of maintenance. It is highly likely that by the time the next edition of this book comes out videotape recording, analog or digital, will be a thing of the past.

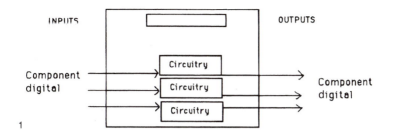

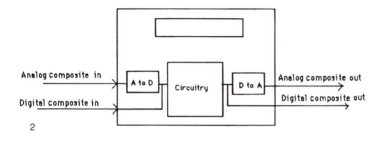

1. Component digital only videotape recorder.

2. Digital VTR capable of recording or playing back analog or composite digital video.

# Digital Video Servers

### Problems of Videotape

Videotape recorders, in one form or another, have been around for about 50 years and have served the industry well. They are used in all aspects of video production: acquiring original footage, editing, and playing back programs and commercials. The biggest problem with videotape machines is that they break down frequently and require a lot of maintenance. If a tape machine breaks down instead of showing a scheduled commercial, the station won't get paid for that commercial. Broadcasters would welcome a more reliable machine with an equal or better picture and sound quality, if it doesn't cost too much.

### Video Servers

That machine is here, and it is the *digital video server*. A video server closely resembles a group of computer hard disk drives. With digital compression it is possible to squeeze a great deal of video and audio information onto hard drives. One big difference between computer hard drives and video servers is that servers have several channels so that people can do different things at the same time. With your computer drive you can save a document or you can open something, but those tasks have to be done separately and only by your computer (unless they are networked, which is something else). With a video server one person could be storing still images for later work, while at the same time someone else is playing back an edited piece of video from the same server. The number of people who can work simultaneously on a server is dependent on the number of channels it has. A two-channel server would allow two jobs to be done at the same time, whereas a four-channel server would allow four jobs to be performed at the same time.

Servers can be used for playing back commercials. They can be hooked up to a nonlinear editor and used for storage. They can be used for recording video in the studio. Just about anything you could do with a videotape machine can be done with a video server. Some studios have moved to a "tapeless" environment where videotape is not used at all; everything is done on video servers. In some cases, videotape is still used in the field to acquire original footage. When back in the studio, the tape will be dubbed to the server for editing and processing. With the introduction of disc-based camcorders, however, tape is no longer needed for field acquisition.

Servers have become very affordable in recent years. This change, coupled with the fact that servers are much more reliable than videotape machines and that a station will not have to buy videotape, makes digital video servers a real option for many stations.

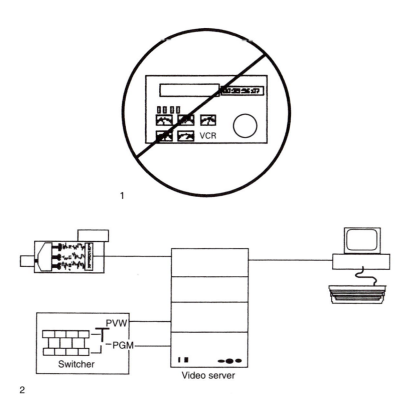

1. Tape is on its way out.

2. Digital video server.

**109**

# Disc-Based Recorders

In the digital world, videotape recorders have two major problems. First, when tape is downloaded into a computer for editing, it must be done in real time. That means if you have an hour of video, it will take an hour to digitize it into the computer. The second problem is that videotape machines tend to break down and require quite a bit of maintenance.

To deal with these problems, manufacturers have started to introduce disc-based recorders. Some of these machines are designed to be installed in a studio, and others are part of self-contained camcorders. Some of the machines use magnetic discs similar to the hard drives in your computer. Others use discs similar to recordable DVDs. Some of the discs are permanently mounted, and others are removable. Whatever the method used, these machines offer two big advantages over videotape machines. First, they are much more reliable. Second, they interface with computers better. The removable discs can be popped into a player in the computer and be used much like a DVD. The nonremovable disc units can be plugged into a computer port, and the computer will recognize and use it just like it was another hard drive. In either case the need to download material in real time is eliminated.

At the time of this writing these machines are still relatively new. Expect them to become more and more common as time goes on.

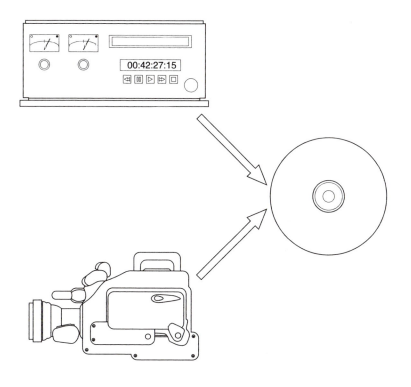

**Both studio machines and field camcorders can be disc recorders.**

**111**

# Editing Analog Videotape

### Physical Cutting and Splicing

In the early days of videotape, editing was a difficult and time-consuming process. A liquid solution had to be put on the tape to make the control track oxide patterns visible. The tape had to be viewed under magnification, and then it was physically cut. Finally, the ends were spliced together with a special tape. The roughness that the splice created in the tape's surface often damaged or even destroyed the tape head. Needless to say, editing tape was done only when there was no other alternative.

### Electronic Editing

Today video editing is done electronically. Information that should be sequential may be out of order on one tape, or it may be distributed among several different tapes. During editing, the material is recorded electronically in the proper sequence onto another tape. The process of copying information from one tape to another is called *dubbing*. Whenever we dub a tape, we drop a generation. The original tape that the video is recorded onto is called the master or first-generation tape. If we make a copy of that tape, it is a second-generation tape. If a dub is made of the second-generation tape, the resulting tape becomes a third-generation tape, and so on.

Every generation drop also entails a loss of quality. The signal has to go through the entire electronics of a tape recorder, be recorded onto the tape, taken off the tape, and run to another tape recorder. Every step of this process adds more noise to the signal and diminishes the original quality of the signal. A top-rated VTR can go several generations before this quality loss becomes visible to the human eye. However, a low-quality machine, such as a home VTR, will show a very visible quality loss on a second-generation tape. (You may refer to your home machine as a VCR which stands for videocassette recorder. VTR is short for videotape recorder, so VTR applies to all videotape machines while VCR applies to only those machines that have the tape contained in a plastic enclosure.)

Editing allows you to shoot a video production in the most efficient manner, which often means shooting scenes out of sequence from the script. These disconnected scenes can then be rearranged and put together in sequence in the editing suite. The second figure shows the master tape, with the shots in nonsequential order. Through the editing process, the shots or scenes are arranged into their proper sequence.

**112**

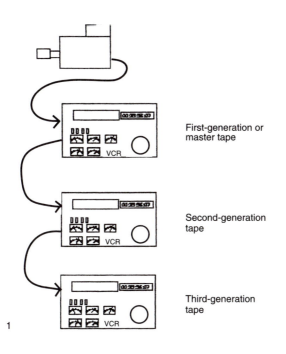

First-generation or master tape

Second-generation tape

Third-generation tape

1

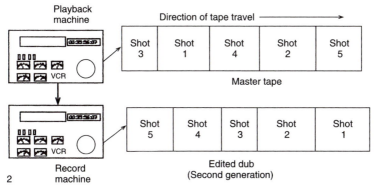

Playback machine

Direction of tape travel ⟶

| Shot 3 | Shot 1 | Shot 4 | Shot 2 | Shot 5 |

Master tape

| Shot 5 | Shot 4 | Shot 3 | Shot 2 | Shot 1 |

Edited dub
(Second generation)

Record machine

2

1. **Tape generations.**

2. **Tape editing.**

*The basis of editing is putting two shots together.*

# The Editing Process (1)

It will be helpful to step through several edits made on a basic editing system just to become familiar with some concepts of the process. You begin with the master tape (containing the shots in nonsequential order), a blank tape, and the VTRs on which to run them; the playback VTR, which will run the master tape; and the record VTR, with which edits will be recorded on the blank tape. First, you find the beginning and end points of the first shot, also called *edit points*, and stop the master tape in the playback machine at the beginning of that shot. Preparing a tape for editing in this manner is called *cueing up the tape*. This is the first step in recording the first shot onto the blank tape.

The motors in each VTR must be at full speed and have achieved their full level of lockup before accurate recording can begin. Most modern editing machines take about half a second to reach full speed and lockup. This is not much time, but it is still 15 frames. Thus, rather than beginning the recording process at the first edit point, you must start the VTRs approximately half a second before this point. This is called *prerolling the VTRs*. You stop the machines when the edit has been fully recorded onto the blank tape.

You then locate the edit points for the second shot on the master tape. The beginning of the second edit is cued up on the playback VTR, and the tape in the record VTR is stopped at the end of the first edit. Both machines are prerolled and then started in the playback mode. At the precise instant the playback and record VTRs reach, respectively, the beginning of the second edit and the end of the first, the record VTR is switched into the record mode. After the second edit is fully recorded, both machines are stopped and the entire process can be reviewed. You should be viewing shot one with a sharp, clean cut to shot two at the right moment.

You go through the same process for the rest of the shots in your show. This is how you build scenes into sequences and sequences into final shows.

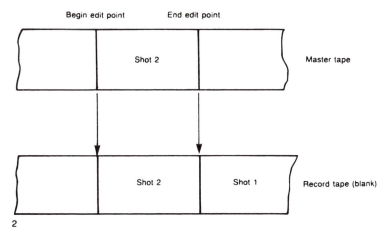

Begin edit point      End edit point

Shot 2      Master tape

Shot 2      Shot 1      Record tape (blank)

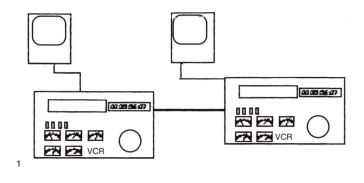

1.   **Manual editing.**

2.   **A typical video edit. A segment of tape is recorded from a master tape to its proper position on the record tape.**

# The Editing Process (2)

The process just described on the previous page concerns by far the most basic edit possible and uses the most rudimentary equipment. The more advanced and precise editing systems and methods are, the more complex the means by which video information is organized, accessed, and transferred into a sequence.

In a very basic system such as that described, the operator may unscientifically gauge when to make cuts and punch the specific button where he or she wants material to be copied. In advanced systems, such tasks are electronically programmed into a computer and precisely executed according to extremely accurate timing systems.

On longer videos especially, the editing process can be quite complicated. A crucial part of most editing tasks is the editing script or *EDL (edit decision list)*. An EDL is a list of the shots you want to use, in the order in which you want to use them. The EDL will include the beginning and ending points of each shot. In very basic systems, these points may be specific visual or aural references, and you may need to manually time the length of each edit. Advanced systems have special coding systems by which you can designate the edit points.

Although creating an edit script may require a good deal of time, having a good script before you begin to make the edits will save you a great deal of effort. Ideally, most of your editing decisions will have been made ahead of time by reviewing the tapes, so that you will have less to worry about when you sit down to actually make the edits.

Program:_____  Date:_____

Producer:_____  Writer:_____

Director:_____  Editor:_____

| Segment | Description | Source | Edit In Hr. Min. Sec. Fr. | Edit Out Hr. Min. Sec. Fr. | Duration Hr. Min. Sec. Fr. | Transition |
|---------|-------------|--------|---------------------------|----------------------------|----------------------------|------------|
|  |  |  |  |  |  |  |
|  |  |  |  |  |  |  |
|  |  |  |  |  |  |  |
|  |  |  |  |  |  |  |
|  |  |  |  |  |  |  |
|  |  |  |  |  |  |  |
|  |  |  |  |  |  |  |
|  |  |  |  |  |  |  |
|  |  |  |  |  |  |  |
|  |  |  |  |  |  |  |
|  |  |  |  |  |  |  |
|  |  |  |  |  |  |  |
|  |  |  |  |  |  |  |
|  |  |  |  |  |  |  |
|  |  |  |  |  |  |  |
|  |  |  |  |  |  |  |

**EDL form.**

*Assemble and insert edits to give you more creative options.*

# Types of Edits

### Assemble Edits

The two basic types of edits are assemble edits and insert edits. With *assemble edits*, you start with a blank tape to record on. When you make the edits onto that tape, everything is recorded from the master tape: audio, video, and control track. Since the control track is coming off the playback machine rather than from the sync generator, the interval between pulses may be off (because of time base error), and the pulses themselves will be degraded (because of the generation drop). Because of these problems, the images may break up on the monitor when the edit is played back. The advantage of assemble editing is that it takes no advance preparation of the tape, but there may be problems in getting good, clean edits.

### Insert Edits

*Insert edits*, on the other hand, require some preparation of the recording tape before editing begins. In order to do insert edits, a control track must be laid down first. This is usually done by placing a blank tape into a VTR, punching up black on the switcher, and putting the machine in record for the entire length of the tape. This will record a black video on the video tracks and lay down the control track pulses from the sync generator.

Now you are ready to do insert edits, and insert edits give you a couple of advantages. First, you can edit using the procedure outlined above, but since the machine is using good, clean, consistent control track pulses, the edits are less likely to break up. Second, you can insert new material over old material. Assume that you had tape of a person talking about a terrific new invention. The audio information is interesting, but the video of a talking head is boring. So you take interesting video that you have of the invention (called B-roll material) and insert just that video over the boring talking head. Now, you have the interesting audio information as well as a visually interesting picture to look at. You could also insert new audio without changing the video you laid down previously. You can go either way. But the key thing to remember is that to do insert editing, the control track must be laid down on the tape you intend to edit to.

**118**

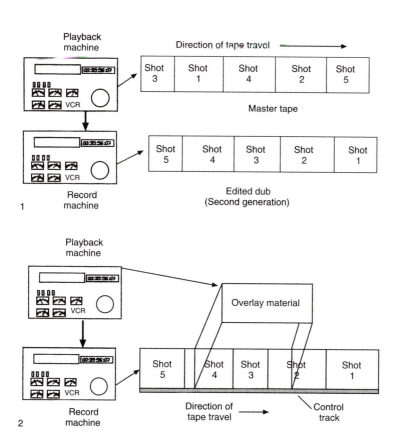

1. **Assemble edits.**

2. **Insert edits.**

*To be edited, video must have a structure.*

# Editing Methods — Manual

There are three basic methods of controlling and editing videotape: manual, control track, and SMPTE time code.

### Manual Editing

*Manual editing* was described in the earlier section, "The Editing Process." You select and make edits based on visual or aural edit points. If, after prerolling both playback and record VTRs and placing them in playback mode, you decide the edit points are not coinciding as you'd like, you can abort the edit by not switching the record VTR to record mode. You can then change the amount of preroll on one or both tapes and try again. This is obviously a rather inaccurate and time-consuming way to edit, but sometimes it's the only choice.

This method of editing is almost never used today. In the earliest days of videotape editing it was the only method available. As new technologies for controlling the editing process became available and affordable, manual editing died out. It is, however, helpful to understand the process because newer edit controllers are executing the same process, but they are executing the process much more quickly and accurately.

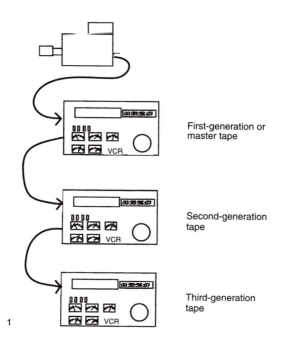

First-generation or master tape

Second-generation tape

Third-generation tape

1

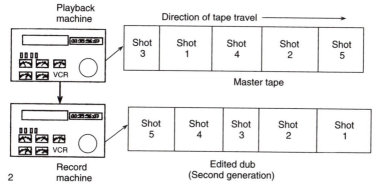

Playback machine

Direction of tape travel ⟶

| Shot 3 | Shot 1 | Shot 4 | Shot 2 | Shot 5 |

Master tape

| Shot 5 | Shot 4 | Shot 3 | Shot 2 | Shot 1 |

Record machine

2

Edited dub (Second generation)

1. **Tape generations.**

2. **Tape editing.**

# Editing Methods — Control Track Counters

A better method is to use a *control track counter editing system*. As noted earlier in "Other Tracks and Lockup (2)," vertical sync pulses are laid down regularly on the control track to stabilize the tape's playback speed. A control track counter editing system uses these pulses as reference points to simulate and perform edits.

The control track counter is hooked up between the VTRs, although some systems have a counter built in. This editing process begins much as the manual method does. You select edit points on the playback and record machines. However, the editing system usually prerolls the machines for you and offers a preview option. If you select this mode, the system prerolls the machines and starts them, displaying first the output from the record machine (the previous shot) and then, at the correct edit point, switching to the playback machine's output (the current shot). This simulates the edit without actually making it. If the edit was good, you can have the system make the edit that was previewed.

This sounds like a pretty incredible machine, but it operates on a very simple principle. The heart of this editing system, the edit controller, merely counts control track pulses. So once the edit point is chosen, all it does is count pulses. When the controller backs up the machines for preroll, it backs up both machines the same number of pulses, then rolls forward, counting the pulses, until it gets to the original edit points, at which point it makes the edit.

The controller ends the edit in the same way. Based on the end points that you predetermined, the controller measures the duration of the edit by counting the number of pulses. When you finally initiate the edit, the controller can recount the pulses and properly end the edit.

Since the controller is counting control track pulses, control track must be laid down in the areas the controller engages. This is particularly important in assemble editing when you are adding a shot. The control track pulses at the very end of an edit (in the last few frames) may not be of good quality because the controller has already begun to end the edit. If your end point is exactly where you want the edit to end, the next edits in point may be either in an area of poor pulses or where there are no pulses at all. Therefore, when you are assemble editing, always let a scene continue longer than you need to; your next edit still can begin where you want it and you will have good pulses for the in point.

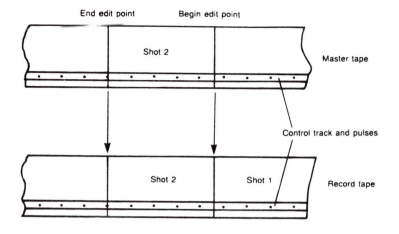

End edit point    Begin edit point

Shot 2

Master tape

Control track and pulses

Shot 2    Shot 1

Record tape

**An edit made using a control track system. The system determines the length of the edit by counting control track pulses.**

*In order to get broadcast-quality tape, edit with SMPTE time code.*

# SMPTE Time Code Editing

One of the problems of the editing methods discussed earlier is that it is difficult to make an accurate editing script or edit decision list (EDL). An EDL is a list of the scenes you want to use in the order in which you want to use them. You would list the beginning point of each scene and the ending point of each scene. The problem is how to record, accurately, what the scenes are. If you describe the beginning and ending points, you still have to search through the tape to find that particular scene. If you did several takes of the same scene, which one do you use? Or you could use the numbers on the tape machine counter. The problem here is that the counters are not accurate. Every time you take a tape off the machine and put it back on the numbers will change. The solution to this problem is *SMPTE (Society of Motion Picture and Television Engineers) time code.* SMPTE time code uses one of the audio tracks or a special address track that many formats have to lay down a specific code number for each frame of video information on the tape. This code consists of a time; for example, 00:27:14:03 would be read as 0 hour, 27 minutes, 14 seconds, and 3 frames. This system works well partly because there are 30 video frames per second.

Since each tape would normally start at 00:00:00:00, the above address would be almost halfway into an hour tape. The address is permanent. If the tape is taken off the machine and stored for a few years, 00:27:14:03 is going to be at exactly the same place on the tape coming out of the vault as it was when the tape went into the vault. Since many professional tapes are no more than an hour long, the hours column of the time code is generally used to identify the tape. For example, a time code of 05:36:56:24 would normally be 36 minutes, 56 seconds, and 24 frames into tape number 5.

The first advantage of SMPTE time code is that it makes putting together an editing script much easier and faster. With SMPTE time code, when you find the beginning or ending edit point, you simply write down the time code number. You don't have to write down a description of the aural or visual cues that indicate the edit points. Thus, it's much faster to go through a tape and put together an editing script. This is particularly important if the video is very long and/or complex, such as a television program.

Editing by SMPTE time code is much more expensive, but it is also much more precise and reliable. For this reason, and because the code enables you to more easily organize and manipulate large amounts of material, most broadcast tapes are edited using time code.

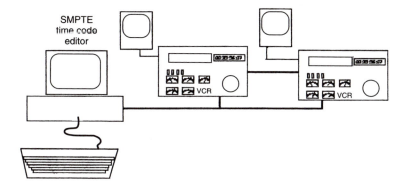

**SMPTE time code editor.**

# Off-Line and On-Line Editing

SMPTE time code also makes on-line and off-line editing practical and economical. A top of the line, full-blown editing suite can easily cost over $1 million to build, while an editing suite using a smaller format might cost less than a quarter of that. The rental fees of such suites will reflect the difference in costs. So it's going to cost a lot more (five or six times as much) to do all your work in the expensive suite than if you could do most of your work in the less expensive suite and spend only a little time in the high-end suite. This is what on-line and off-line editing lets you do. To begin with, when you first record your show on high-quality tape, you also record it on small-format tape and lay down the same time codes on the two tapes.

## Off-Line Editing

During this phase you put your high-quality tape in a storage vault and take your small-format tape to its editing suite and start developing your editing script by viewing the tape and selecting the order and edit points of the video segments you wish to join. As you develop the script, you also edit the tape. This will be your work print. Developing your editing script and work print is the most time-consuming part of the editing process. You don't really care about the quality of the tape because no one else is going to see it. Its primary purpose is to allow you to see how the edits fit together so that you can finalize your editing script. Putting together your editing script and your small-format work print that no one else is going to see is called *off-line editing*.

## On-Line Editing

Putting together the large-format final tape is called *on-line editing*. After you finish the work print and the editing script, you retrieve your high-quality tape from the vault and go to the editing suite. The final, high-quality tape is easy to put together because during off-line editing you determined the specific end points and order of every edit. Since the time code numbers are the same for both tapes, you can simply use your final editing script numbers to edit on-line.

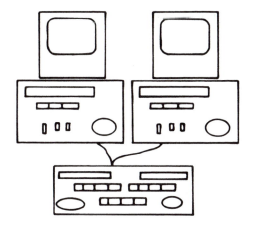

Off-line editing.

*Computers help coordinate the editing process.*

# Editing by Computer

The real beauty of SMPTE time code editing is that special edit controller computers can do most of the work for you. The most sophisticated of these machines can control several tape machines and a programmable switcher at the same time. With more than one playback machine (provided they're properly time base corrected), you can dissolve, wipe, key, and do other effects between machines. All of this can be entered into the edit controller, and it will do everything: cue and preroll the machines, command the switcher to do special effects between the machines, and have the record machine do the actual edits. All you have to do is program the computer properly by entering the editing script containing all the scenes in sequence designated by SMPTE time code.

### Drop Frame/Non-Drop Frame Editing
Throughout this book, in order to keep things simple and understandable, a frame rate of 30 frames and 60 fields per second has been used. That is not exactly accurate, however. In order to add the color information to the luminance information, a slightly different frame rate is required. In reality, the NTSC system has 59.94 fields and 29.97 frames per second. For our needs up to now, this has not been a problem. But when dealing with SMPTE time code it does create a problem. Since SMPTE time code uses 30 frames per second when there are only 29.97 frames per second, the timing will be off before you get very far into the tape. By the end of the program, SMPTE time code will show your program to be a different length than it really is. To compensate for this problem, time code generators and editors will allow either a *drop frame mode* or a *non-drop frame mode* to be selected. In the drop frame mode, at selected places the system will drop a frame so that a second of time will only have 29 frames instead of 30 frames. This will keep the time code of a program and the actual time of the program the same. In the non-drop frame mode the time code and the actual length of the program will be different. You will need to decide which mode works best for your particular situation.

These computer-controlled systems can do remarkable things, but you have to keep one thing in mind. The computer can carry out your commands accurately, but it takes the creativity and organization of a person to create, develop, and refine the show's idea and execution.

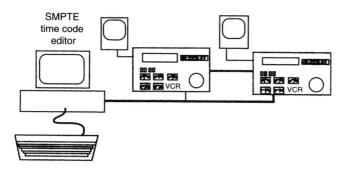

SMPTE Time Code Editor

Actual Running Time of Tape = SMPTE Time Code Time

Actual Running Time of Tape Does Not = SMPTE Time Code Time

# Problems of Traditional Editing

Although SMPTE time code and computerized editors have greatly enhanced the editing process, there is a problem that limits flexibility and creativity in traditional editing, particularly in off-line editing. Once you have edited a sequence of scenes together, you cannot go back and change one of those scenes without reediting the entire tape from that point on. Assume, for example, that you had edited a tape with four scenes in it. After looking at the tape several times, you decide that the tape would be much better if the second scene started two seconds earlier. That will make the second scene and the tape two seconds longer. If you go back and reedit that scene and include the extra two seconds, the new scene will overlap and blank out the first two seconds of the third scene. As a result, you will have to reedit the third scene, which will now overlap the fourth scene. So you will have to reedit that. If you were to take that second scene and cut it down by two seconds, instead of adding two seconds, there would be unwanted material on the tape between the end of the new scene two and the beginning of scene three. So, again, the tape would have to be reedited from the new end of scene two. Imagine how much more complex and time consuming the problem would be if you had to make a change early in a half-hour program that had 45 or more edits. This traditional process is called *linear editing* and, as you can imagine, is very time consuming. Since you will be renting the editing suite, that additional time translates into an increased expense.

One advantage of off-line editing is that it allows you to go through this process and develop an EDL using relatively inexpensive small-format equipment. Imagine how much more time and money could be saved if you did not have to go back and completely reedit a tape after changing a scene.

Since the beginning of videotape editing in the early 1970s, engineers have been trying to devise editing systems that would allow you to make changes wherever you want without requiring you to go back and reedit the entire piece. Those systems were developed in the mid-1990s. They will be discussed next.

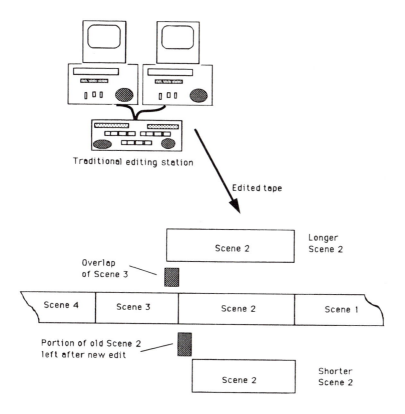

Traditional editing station

Edited tape

Longer
Scene 2

Scene 2

Overlap
of Scene 3

| Scene 4 | Scene 3 | Scene 2 | Scene 1 |

Portion of old Scene 2
left after new edit

Scene 2

Shorter
Scene 2

**Problems of reediting a tape using traditional methods.**

# Nonlinear Editing

The advent of digital video and of new, more powerful small computers has brought about what is called *nonlinear editing*. This allows the editor to go back and change or modify individual scenes at any time without the need to reedit the entire tape from that point on.

The process can vary a little. With some formats the digital video can be transferred directly from the recorder to the editor. Analog videotape will have to be digitized and stored in a digital memory. Some digital tape formats will also have to be dubbed to the editor in real time.

Using a powerful computer with specialized programming, the editor can call up individual shots and scenes from that memory. As the editor views the material, he or she can decide how long each shot should be and in what order the shots should be played back. When playing back an edited scene, the computer calls up the first shot chosen from its memory and displays the selected segment. It then calls up the next shot selected and displays it, and so on. What the editor is actually seeing is selected segments of the computer memory displayed one after the other in a continuous manner. This will appear as a single uninterrupted scene. The editor can put together the entire program in this way. If the editor wants to change a scene, he or she just goes back to that portion of the playback and makes whatever additions or cuts are desired. When playing back the changed sequence, the computer will include the changes and play back the subsequent scene at the proper time.

In this way, the editor can do a "rough cut" of the entire show and then go back and fine-tune or polish the rough spots without having to reedit the entire segment. Once the editor is satisfied with the show, the edit decision list can be put together for the on-line editing of the show.

Since some videotape formats require that the video be digitized and stored in a digital memory, there is an added step that requires some time that is not necessary using a video server or other disc-based sources. Once the video is in memory, however, greater creativity and flexibility are possible. Nonlinear editing has almost completely replaced traditional linear tape editing.

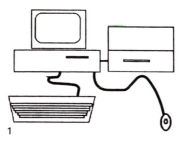

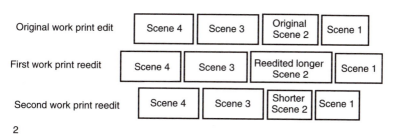

| Original work print edit | Scene 4 | Scene 3 | Original Scene 2 | Scene 1 |
|---|---|---|---|---|
| First work print reedit | Scene 4 | Scene 3 | Reedited longer Scene 2 | Scene 1 |
| Second work print reedit | Scene 4 | Scene 3 | Shorter Scene 2 | Scene 1 |

2

1. **Personal computer-based off-line nonlinear editing station.**

2. **Flexibility of nonlinear editing.**

*Information can be squeezed into a smaller space.*

# Video Compression

Digital video can take up an enormous amount of signal bandwidth, whether it is going down a cable or being transmitted over the air. *Video compression* allows that information to be compressed into a smaller bandwidth. When you are dealing with a limited amount of space (or bandwidth) the ability to compress more information into less space is a real advantage.

One great advantage of digital video is that it is much easier to manipulate and modify than analog information. Since the digital video signal is made up of a series of numbers, computer programs and mathematical formulas can be developed to add numbers, change numbers, or subtract numbers, thus adding video, changing video, or subtracting video. This idea is used in the process of video compression.

Compression isn't really an accurate word for what takes place. Compression indicates that a certain amount of information is pushed into a smaller space, and that's not what happens. Actually, compression throws away information. Some compression methods are lossless, which means that the picture quality stays the same. Other methods are lossy which means picture quality is degraded. In reality, since all compression systems throw away information, there is a loss of quality even if you don't see it.

For video there are two parts of the compression process: spatial compression and temporal compression.

1

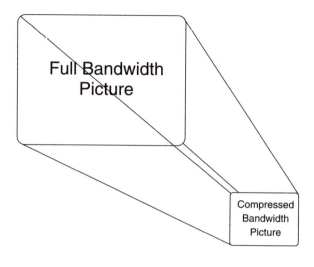

Full Bandwidth Picture

Compressed
Bandwidth
Picture

2

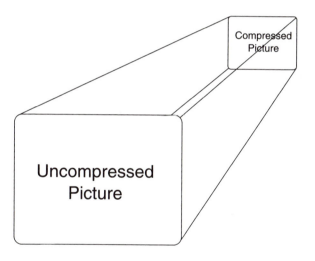

Compressed
Picture

Uncompressed
Picture

**Compression is a two step process:**

1. Compressing to save bandwidth for transmission.

2. Uncompressing for picture display.

# Spatial Compression

Each video frame has lots of redundancy in it. Blue sky, grass, walls, furniture, uniforms, and so on. Spatial compression seeks to eliminate this redundancy and save bandwidth by keeping only the key information. For example, a compression system might chop a video frame into 4 pixel by 4 pixel and 8 pixel by 8 pixel blocks of information. If there is blue sky in those blocks, it might not be necessary to include all of the information from each of the 64 pixels. But the information for one pixel could be sent down the line with a code to repeat the same thing for the other 63 pixels. This would eliminate redundancy and reduce bandwidth requirements.

### Entropy Reduction
Systems will also take information that is not very important and throw it away. This is called *entropy reduction*.

### Entropy Encoding
Another technique uses shorter bit strings to represent commonly used colors and shades and longer bit strings to represent uncommonly used colors and shades. It would be like the computer saying: "Use this 6-bit string to mean this color of red that would normally need 8 bits," and "use this 10-bit string to mean this color of puce that normally requires 8 bits." This technique is called *entropy encoding*.

A number of different mathematical formulas, called *algorithms*, can be used in video compression. In order to make the system work, the transmitting end and the receiving end of the system must be using the same formula. These formulas are always a compromise. If you don't send enough information down the line, the final picture will not be as sharp and clear as it should be. On the other hand, if you are trying to save bandwidth, you don't want to send any more information than you have to.

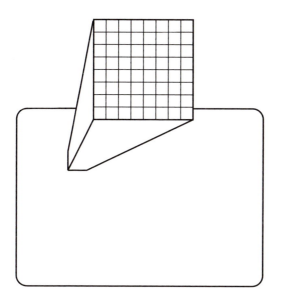

**Some compression is done by using 4 by 4 and 8 by 8 blocks of pixels.**

6 bits

010011

=

8 bits

11010010

10 bits

1010001110

=

8 bits

00011011

**Entropy encoding.**

# Temporal Compression

Although spatial compression removes redundancies from individual frames, there is also a great deal of redundancy from frame to frame. *Temporal compression* deals with this problem. While a number of approaches and very complicated algorithms are used, let's look at the general concept.

In order to understand how temporal compression works, it might be easier to deal with just two individual frames of video, one right after the other. In the first frame, a race car is speeding around the race track. If we look at the next frame of video, which happens only one one-thirtieth of a second later, the two frames are almost identical. Things have moved a little, but in such a short period of time not very much can change. Using video compression, the system would send the first frame down the line where it would be both displayed and held in a memory. But instead of sending all of the information of the second frame, the system would send only the information that was different from that in the first frame. On the receiving end, a computer program would take the information from the first frame that has not changed and combine it with the new information from the second frame. This new second frame would then be displayed and stored in the memory, where the process would start over again with just the new information for the third frame coming down the line. You can see that this process would greatly reduce the amount of information being transmitted at any one time, but it would require much more sophisticated equipment at both the transmitting and receiving ends.

Compression is often described by its compression ratio. It might be spoken of as 2:1 (two to one) compression or 4:1 (four to one) compression. What this means is that if you take the bandwidth it takes to carry one complete uncompressed video signal, with 4:1 compression you could fit four complete video signals in that same bandwidth. The higher the compression ratio, the greater the expectation of poor quality in the final picture.

Video compression can be used almost anywhere video information has to be stored (whether on tape or on some sort of computer memory device), or for transmitting information through cable or over the air. But compression is always a compromise. Many professionals hate the "C" word (compression) because it means compromise and loss of information. Compression is a fact of life, however, and many nonlinear editors and digital video recording formats would be unable to function without it.

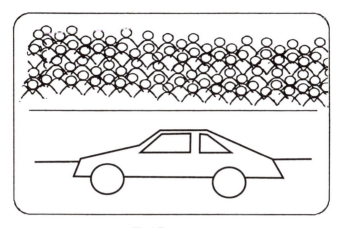

**First Frame**

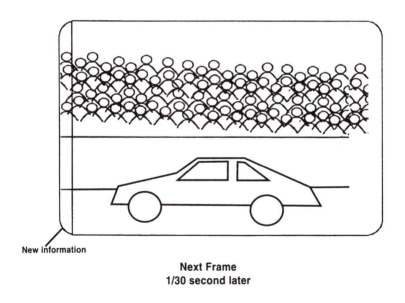

New information

**Next Frame**
**1/30 second later**

Video compression.

# MPEG Compression Standard

The current standard for video compression was created by the Moving Pictures Experts Group (*MPEG*). The MPEG organization has come up with several compression standards for video, Internet, sound, and others. You are probably familiar with their compression standard for sound. The MP standard, as it is frequently referred to, is frequently used for computer music files.

The compression standards for video are called *MPEG 2*. They include both spatial and temporal compression methods to make the most efficient use of bandwidth. The designers of this standard realized that consumers couldn't go out and buy a new decoder every time advances were made in the technology. So they set up MPEG as a protocol. As long as the compressed material fit the protocol, it could be decoded by the MPEG decoder no matter what algorithm was used to compress the video. This allowed more complex compression algorithms to be developed and higher compression ratios to be established without the need to change the equipment on the consumer's end of the chain.

An example is the home satellite systems. When they first came on the market, MPEG 2 allowed them to compress movies at a 4:1 ratio. Within a few years they were compressing movies at an 8:1 ratio with no change in the consumer's receivers. MPEG is pretty much the standard for quality video compression in the broadcast world.

MPEG encoders.

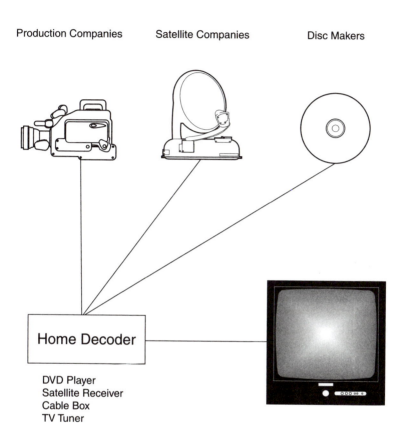

Production Companies       Satellite Companies          Disc Makers

Home Decoder

DVD Player
Satellite Receiver
Cable Box
TV Tuner

# Computer Graphics for Video

### Originating Computer Graphics

As you have already learned, digital video is really a series of 0s and 1s representing distinct voltages; the numbers are converted back to distinct voltages to form analog video. So, if you could sit down at a computer terminal and enter a long series of 0s and 1s, you would have just created a frame of video information. Needless to say, this would take a high degree of technical training and knowledge, as well as being a very time-consuming and tedious way to do things. What is needed is a method of creating digital video images that would be as simple as typing at a computer or drawing with a pencil and paper.

### Interface between People and Machines

A number of digital graphic systems have been developed that enable a person to take advantage of the opportunities offered by digital video. The capabilities of these systems range from producing simple letters and numbers to creating complex, detailed original illustrations and manipulating images on the screen. These systems provide an interface between the process of entering a series of numbers and the person who needs to get a job done. There are two things needed to make these interfaces successful. First, they must operate in a manner similar to what the user is already familiar with. If someone is introduced to a new piece of equipment that has several familiar features, he or she won't be as intimidated by it. But if a new piece of equipment is totally foreign, people will be more reluctant to try it out. Second, this new equipment needs to be flexible. The more that can be done with it, the more attractive it will be.

1. To effectively create a picture (or frame of video) on a computer, you might have had to enter thousands and thousands of values.

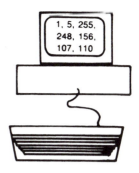

1, 5, 255, 248, 156, 107, 110

1

2

2. Fortunately, computers can translate our general commands into these thousands of specific values. We deliver these commands to the computer in simple ways, such as through a keyboard, an electronic "pencil and paper," or even voice.

# Character Generators

*Character generators (CGs)* were the first digital graphics units. A CG looks something like a computer terminal. It is, in fact, intended to be used like a word processor. Many of the editing features now used on electronic word processing systems were first used on CGs. CGs allow you to type titles onto the TV screen. If you want to make credits for who wrote, produced, directed, and starred in the show, use the CG. If you're interviewing someone and you want to flash a name up on the screen so the viewers know who the person is, use the CG.

The earliest CGs were very simple. They only produced white lettering on black background for use as "keys." There were one or two type sizes, and only one or two type styles (fonts). But now you can do white on black lettering, or you can give the letters any color you want and produce a colored background. You can make the letters an outline, or solid, or solid with an outline. There's a wide variety of sizes and fonts available; the range is amazing. To be most effective, character generators also need to have an extensive memory. CG memories used to be measured in pages. One complete video frame of information was a page. When titles were just simple lettering it was easy to define the number of pages in the memory. With the addition of colors, shadows, outlines, and movement, the memory needed to make up a page varies with the complexity of the image. Pages are no longer a valid way to measure character generator memory. Today, we measure CG memory just as we would for any other computer. If you're preparing a show that has opening titles, names inserted during the show, and closing credits, you're going to need a lot of information. If the show is shot live, this is too much to be typed as it's needed. However, you can enter all the information into the CG's memory before the show begins. Then it can be brought out of the memory when needed. Of course, what is really happening is that the CG is generating a series of numbers. But the main control unit will still look very much like a standard computer terminal.

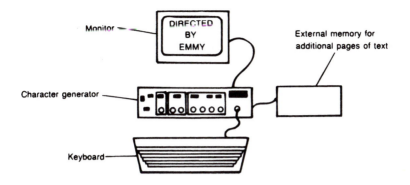

**Components of a typical character generator.**

*Draw and paint on video.*

# Creating Imagery and Effects

### Computer-Generated Imagery (CGI)
As the name implies, these digital graphics devices allow you to easily compose drawings or combinations of illustrations and text that can be manipulated and reproduced in a number of different forms, including on paper and as part of a video. These electronic graphic systems look very much like computers. There is the terminal, with the monitor (maybe two) and the disc drives, but there is also something that looks like a pencil and paper. It isn't a real pencil and paper, of course, but an electronic palette and stylus. Most of the work is done with the palette and stylus. Some systems just use a mouse in place of the stylus and palette.

The palette looks like a flat rectangular piece of plastic with a wire coming out of it. The stylus looks like a rather fat ballpoint pen with a wire coming out of the top of it. The monitor displays a rectangular image area and menu boxes (lists of commands by which the computer receives instructions). When the point of the pen is touched to the palette, a cross usually appears on the monitor. As the point of the pen is moved across the palette, a corresponding line appears in the image area of the screen. So, while you draw on the palette, the image doesn't appear there but rather on the monitor. You can choose different brush styles and textures, colors, and other details by simply touching the point of the pen to the appropriate menu box on the monitor. The keyboard terminal is used to enter text into the art work, and the finished product can be stored and recalled from memory at will.

Each make and model of the electronic graphics system will have its own features, but most will operate along the lines outlined here. Like the character generator, the system is storing an image as a long stream of numbers that will be converted to analog voltages at the output of the system.

### Digital Video Effects
*Digital video effects (DVE)* systems enable a user to manipulate a digitized video signal and produce any of an incredible array of special effects, such as those described earlier. These devices can be incredibly complex, and the specific operation of different models can vary greatly. However, you should understand the basic concepts underlying their place in any video system. Remember that a DVE still serves as an interface between people and numbers. The video comes out of the switcher and into the DVE, where the video is then modified by the manipulation of knobs, levers, and buttons on the DVE control panel. From there it goes back to the switcher. In a fully digital system or in a digital switcher, there is no need for the conversions between analog and digital.

**146**

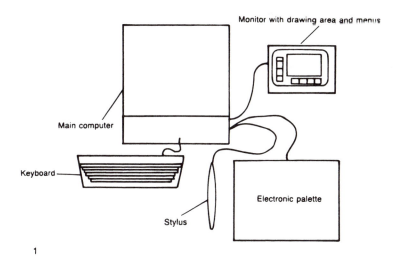

1

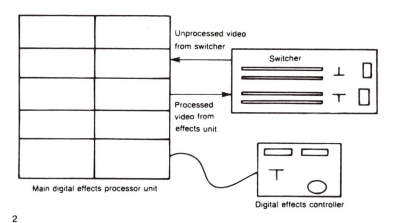

2

1. Typical components of a computer graphics system.

2. Typical digital effects setup.

# The Digital Studio

By this point you may be thinking that there is an awful lot of digital equipment out there, and you would be right. Digital cameras digitize the video information as soon as it comes off of the CCD and send it down the line. Digital distribution amplifiers can send that digital signal to several different destinations. Digital switchers allow you to select, process, and manipulate the digital signal. Character generators, computer-generated imagery equipment, nonlinear editors, and video servers are all digital pieces of equipment. If analog video isn't dead, it is certainly on its last legs. More and more completely digital studios are being built.

A completely *digital studio* is one in which you start with digital cameras and the signal remains in digital form right to and including the transmitter. The only piece of analog equipment that might remain in the studio, or the home for that matter, will be the CRT displaying the images. But if your final display will be on a plasma display screen, even that is digital. So the signal will be digital throughout the complete process unless it reaches the CRT where it will be converted to analog for final display.

The process of fully converting to digital is occurring faster in large markets and is moving at a slower pace in smaller markets. It is going to cost a lot of money, probably several million dollars for each station. Many stations in the largest markets have already made the change. Stations in smaller markets are taking more time and are purchasing more digital equipment as time goes on until it will be a relatively simple matter to complete the conversion. It is harder to predict what will happen with schools because money is always in short supply.

Eventually, everyone will have to make the conversion to a completely digital system because in not too many years analog video equipment will no longer be manufactured.

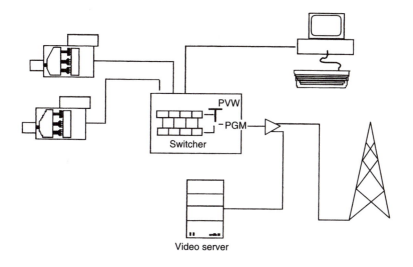

Video server

**The digital studio.**

*A whole new world of desktop video is opening up.*

# Open Architecture Equipment versus Dedicated Equipment

*Dedicated equipment* means that each piece of equipment is dedicated to one specific job, such as a switcher or a character generator.

Many companies, instead of designing a piece of equipment to do one specific job, such as a character generator, are starting with a computer and writing special programs that will allow that computer to meet the special needs of video production. Special adapters have to be built to allow the video signal and the computer to be integrated. This type of equipment is called *open architecture equipment* because the computer is not dedicated to any one specific use and is open to many uses, depending on the software (programs) running on the computer. Using this approach, you can start with a high-level home computer and make that computer into a video graphics system, a character generator, a video switcher, a digital video effects unit, or a nonlinear editor — all of this in one home computer. The quality of the work produced by some of these systems is excellent. These systems are usually far less expensive than dedicated pieces of equipment. These two factors cause many experts to predict that the use of dedicated equipment will die out.

The possibilities for open architecture equipment look wonderful. Instead of having to buy many expensive pieces of equipment dedicated to one job each, you could purchase a relatively inexpensive computer with the right software to do it all. What is happening is that the computer industries and video industries are beginning to converge. Almost all production facilities will have a mix of open architecture and dedicated equipment working together. Productions will be made on this equipment that might be sent out over traditional TV or cable. It might also be streamed on the Internet or made into a DVD. All of the production and distribution channels are converging together.

**150**

Traditional editing station   Computer graphics system

1.

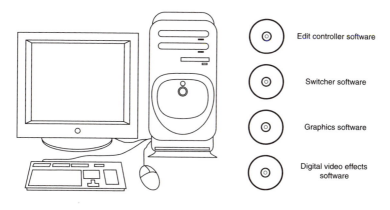

Edit controller software

Switcher software

Graphics software

Digital video effects
software

Computer Station

2.

1. **Dedicated video equipment.**

2. **Open architecture equipment.**

# Drawbacks of Open Architecture Equipment

Open architecture equipment is definitely here to stay, but this type of equipment does have some drawbacks. Because you have one piece of equipment doing many jobs, you have to plan out what you want to do carefully in advance. Open architecture equipment is slower to operate than dedicated equipment. For example, to change cameras on a video switcher you simply have to press a button. With open architecture equipment, you have to enter the instructions through the computer keyboard or with a computer mouse. As a result, dedicated equipment operates more quickly, and the operator can change his or her mind and be more spontaneous with the equipment. The final problem with open architecture equipment is that it operates on computers. And computers, as we all know, can crash at any time for unknown reasons. In postproduction, you have the time to deal with a crashed computer, but if you're doing the Super Bowl live and a team is driving for the winning touchdown with only seconds left, you can't afford to have the whole system crash. Open architecture has pretty well taken over in the postproduction world, but dedicated equipment will have to be used for the foreseeable future for the production of live broadcasts, such as sports and news.

As for the prospect of desktop video, it is a reality. With the introduction of low-cost consumer digital cameras and nonlinear editing programs for under $1000, a person could set up a system for under $5000, and $10,000 will get you a very good-quality system. Many see this as a wonderful development that will allow almost anyone to produce their own shows and have their voices heard. There are some flaws in this theory, however. Just because you have the technology to put together a program doesn't mean you have the skills and experience to tell your story effectively. People have watched thousands of hours of well-produced TV. They have certain expectations in storytelling and production values. If you can't reach a certain level of expertise in telling your story with a professional look and sound, people may not watch. If you put a show together and no one watches, what's the point?

1. Open architecture equipment can crash when you need it most.

2. Open architecture equipment is slower to operate than dedicated equipment making it seem like you need more hands to get the job done.

# High-Definition TV

As good as many of the new systems are, they still leave something to be desired. You may have seen very large-screen TVs and noticed that their pictures weren't as sharp and clear as those for smaller TV sets. That's because you have the same 525 lines spread out over a much larger area. Any time you spread a given amount of information over a larger area, it's not going to look as sharp and clear, even in digital formats. This demonstrates how much quality is lacking in a TV picture, compared to film. For many years there has been a great deal of research and development of TV systems that would produce a picture that approaches film quality. This is called *high-definition television (HDTV)*. The early work on HDTV used analog video, but today everything is digital.

## Production HDTV Standards versus Broadcast HDTV Standards

There are two aspects of HDTV: production and broadcast. *Production* is the technology and equipment used to record and create programming. *Broadcasting* is the method of sending that programming through the air, over cable, or via satellite to your home. Under the old NTSC system, the standard for both processes was the same. With the advent of digital technology, the processes can be very different. When the HDTV production standard was developed, a great deal of effort went into designing a system that would make it easy to convert video between the major broadcast standards in the world (NTSC, PAL, PAL-M). What was wanted was a universal system that would allow easy two-way conversion — a format that would be easy to convert from one of the broadcast standards or film to HDTV and easy to convert from HDTV to one of the broadcast standards or film.

The system developed is a component system that uses either 8-bit, 10-bit, or 12-bit processing; either 720 or 1080 scanning lines of 1920 pixels each; has a 16:9 aspect ratio; uses a 4:2:2 encoding ratio; can be scanned at 60 fields/30 frames interlace, 50 fields/25 frames interlace, 30 frames progressive, or 24 frames progressive per second; and requires a total of 60 MHz (30 MHz for the Y channel and 15 MHz each for the R-Y and B-Y channels).

One of the biggest changes for production people will be the 16:9 screen format. The wide-screen format is close to what movies have been using for years and is much wider than the traditional television screen. For sports this wider screen will make it easier to cover more of the field and action. For dramas, comedies, and news, directors and camera people will have more screen to use and will have to use it effectively without looking contrived.

**154**

16:9 Aspect ratio

1080 Scanning lines of 1920 pixels for each line
with 30 frames of interlace scanning
or 24 or 30 frames of progressive scanning.


or 720 Scanning lines of 1280 pixels for each line
with 24, 30, or 60 frames of progressive scanning

**Formats for high-definition digital television.**

# ATSC High-Definition Broadcast Standard

In April 1998 the Federal Communications Commission announced a new digital broadcast standard for the United States. The new standard was developed by the Advanced Television Systems Committee (ATSC) and provided specifications for high-definition television and *standard definition digital television (SDTV)*. SDTV is what you see if you have the mini-satellite dish or digital cable at home. The new system will allow a group of standards that can be received and displayed by all digital TV sets. So if you have an SDTV set, it will receive both SDTV and HDTV and show it all in SDTV. If you have an HDTV set, it will also receive and display all of the digital standards.

The new ATSC system will be a digital system that uses the same amount of bandwidth (6 MHz) as the current NTSC system. The new system supports 18 different digital standards and will have a wide-screen format similar to motion pictures. The format's aspect ratio is 16 units wide by 9 units high, compared to the NTSC's 3 units high by 4 units wide. There will be two HDTV options. One will use 1080 scanning lines of 1920 pixels each. It will have the scanning options of 60 fields/30 frames interlace scanning or 30 or 24 frames of progressive scanning per second. This standard is usually called *1080 i.* (Note that a 1080, 60-frame progressive standard is being tested as this is written.) The other option has 720 scanning lines of 1280 pixels per line and has either 60, 30, or 24 frames of progressive scanning per second. This format is usually called *720 p.*

We have the different scanning rates because some engineers believe that interlace scanning gives the best pictures, especially for very large screens, but progressive scanning is easier to integrate with computers. The 24 frames per second rate makes it easier to integrate with films which are shot at that rate. In the United States, we are in the process of changing over to this standard now.

16:9 Aspect ratio

1080 Scanning lines of 1920 pixels for each line
with 30 frames of interlace scanning
or 24 or 30 frames of progressive scanning.

or 720 Scanning lines of 1280 pixels for each line
with 24, 30, or 60 frames of progressive scanning.

**Formats for high-definition digital television.**

ATSC High-Definition Broadcast Standard

# Standard Definition Digital Television (SDTV)

Broadcasters have had reservations about HDTV because it costs a lot of money to convert to it and they have seen no apparent way to increase their revenues to recover that additional cost. With the development of high-quality digital compression, it is now possible to digitize the standard NTSC video signal and compress it so that four or more signals can fit into one standard NTSC 6-MHz bandwidth channel. This is what happens if you have one of those small mini-dish home satellite systems or digital cable. They send you multiple channels of digital video that have been compressed into one 6-MHz bandwidth. Your set-top receiver converts it to NTSC to display on your home TV. This is *standard definition digital television (SDTV)*. The ATSC digital broadcast standard that has been approved for the United States includes both HDTV and SDTV. The SDTV picture can be in either the standard 4:3 aspect ratio or the wide-screen 16:9 aspect ratio. The two formats are summarized on the facing page.

Using this sort of system, broadcasters could send out multiple programs on their standard TV channel. Instead of having only one program at a time to sell to advertisers, they would have multiple programs that they could sell and they would have the chance to increase their revenues to cover the cost of converting to digital broadcasting.

No one can predict exactly what is going to happen in the future, but the best guess is that stations will use a combination of SDTV and HDTV in their broadcast day. Perhaps during the daytime hours they will provide multiple programs, and during the evening prime time hours and for important sporting events their programming will be in HDTV. New compression algorithms have been developed that allow one HDTV and one SDTV program over the same 6-MHz television channel. Conventional wisdom had predicted that few stations would have their own HDTV production equipment because it costs so much more than SDTV production equipment. Recently, however, the cost of HDTV production equipment has dropped dramatically so that today you can equip a station with HDTV for what SDTV cost just a couple of years ago. With this change HDTV production equipment might be found in just about any TV station.

As a consumer, if you buy a new digital television receiver or set-top converter, you will be able to receive and watch all of the digital formats.

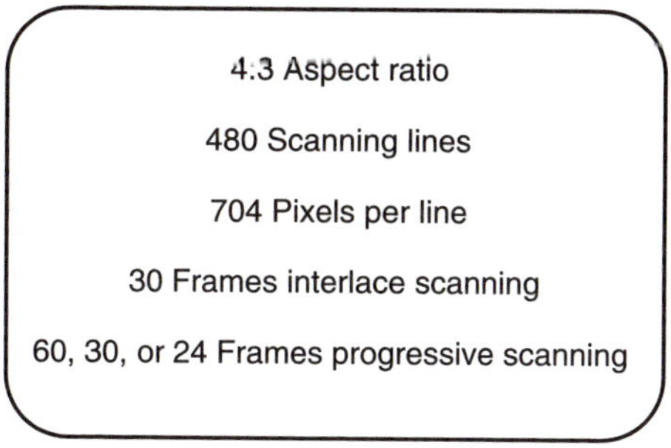

4.3 Aspect ratio

480 Scanning lines

704 Pixels per line

30 Frames interlace scanning

60, 30, or 24 Frames progressive scanning

1

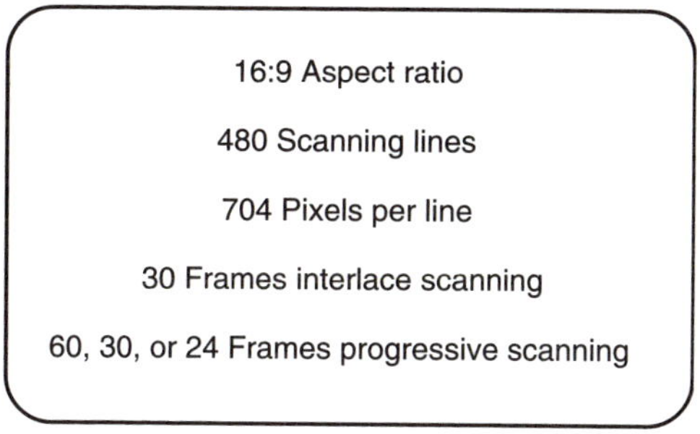

16:9 Aspect ratio

480 Scanning lines

704 Pixels per line

30 Frames interlace scanning

60, 30, or 24 Frames progressive scanning

2

1. **Normal aspect formats for SDTV.**

2. **Wide-screen formats for SDTV.**

*Sound adds a lot to the picture.*

# Audio for Video

In the early years of TV, sound was not considered to be very important. Yes, you had to have sound, but not too much time was spent on it. That thinking has changed dramatically. With so many sources of entertainment and the advent of new sophisticated technology, sound, or audio, has become an important and complex component of any video production.

### The Early Years

Although most people don't listen to music on AM radio today, if you have tuned in to AM, you had have probably noticed that the music doesn't sound as good as the music you listen to on your CD. It doesn't sound as bright or as alive. That's because at the time AM radio was developed the technology wouldn't allow us to record and reproduce the entire range of sounds that the human ear could hear. Sound is vibrations of the air, and the average ear can hear sounds between about 20 Hz and 15,000 Hz (vibrations per second). Early technologies allowed the recording of up to about 5000 Hz, so the brightness and the sparkle of music wasn't recorded and reproduced. In the late 1940s the technology was developed to record the full-frequency range that people can hear. In those days it was called high fidelity or hi-fi. Today full-frequency recording is normal and isn't given much thought.

### Mono and Stereo

Your AM radio is also *monaural* or *mono sound*. Everything is on one channel and comes from one speaker. But we know that sound doesn't come from only one direction. It comes from everywhere. Stereophonic or stereo is a system that gives sound a location. It is sound that seems to come from different locations. Traditional stereo uses two channels and two speakers to carry the complete audio message. If you put one speaker on the left and the other on the right and sit between them, you can get the effect of stereo sound. If you put all of the violins on the left channel and they are played through the left speaker, it will sound like the violins are coming from the left side of the room. If you put all of the trumpets on the right channel and play them through the right speaker, it will sound like the trumpets are coming from the right side of the room. If you record the drums evenly on both channels and play them back on both speakers, it will sound like the drums are coming from the center of the room. If you record the piano so that 60% of its signal is on the left channel and 40% is on the right channel it will sound like the piano is coming from the left of center, but not all the way from the left. With traditional stereo you can place sound anywhere you like between left and right.

**Mono uses one channel of sound through one speaker.**

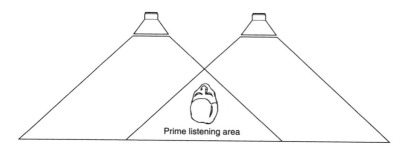

Prime listening area

**Stereo uses two channels of sound through two speakers
to give sound location.**

*Sound can come from anywhere.*

# Surround Sound

Stereo was a great start, but we know that sound can come from anywhere. When you watch a movie in a theater, sound can come from the front, the sides, or behind you. The movies are using *surround sound*, which is another type of stereo. Several channels of sound are played through a number of speakers located around the theater.

### 5.1 Stereo

The new HDTV standard accepted for the United States includes a *5.1 surround sound stereo standard.* Five main speakers are used: left front, center front, right front, right surround, and left surround. If you are seated in the center, sound can be made to come from any part of the room. A center front speaker was added to the traditional left and right speakers in order to create a larger listening envelope where the full effects of the stereo could be heard. These five speaker positions account for the 5 in the 5.1, but what about the .1? The .1 is for what is called a *subwoofer* for very low deep sounds. It is hard to tell exactly where sounds in this range come from, so this speaker can really be placed anywhere.

The 5.1 audio standard will allow the creation of the type of sonic environment that before now was only found in theaters. You may have seen ads for "home theater" systems. Surround sound is a big part of that. While 5.1 provides great creative opportunities, it also creates increased responsibilities for people to learn how to use the opportunities effectively.

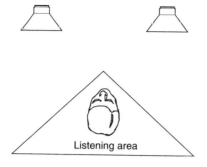

Listening area

**Traditional stereo.**

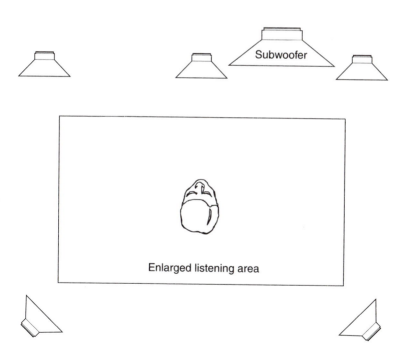

Subwoofer

Enlarged listening area

**5.1 surround sound.**

# Professional and Consumer Audio

### Impedance

Very early in this book we discussed the concept of impedance. In the world of video, life was simple because there was one impedance for everything. It is very different in the world of audio. Consumer video is high impedance (10,000 $\Omega$ (ohms)). High-impedance equipment is less expensive to manufacture, has poorer sound quality, and can only be sent down short cables. Professional equipment is low impedance (600 $\Omega$ or less). Low-impedance equipment has better sound quality, can be sent down longer cables, and is more expensive. There are converters that will change high impedance to low impedance and low to high, but the good ones are fairly expensive.

### Balanced and Unbalanced Audio

Consumer audio is also unbalanced. *Unbalanced audio* uses only two wires to carry the message and does not resist induced noise. (Please see the section on fields (induction) and noise early in the book.) *Balanced audio systems* use three wires to carry the message and resist induced noise. This resistance to noise and, therefore, cleaner signal is the big advantage of balanced audio.

The system works as follows. Of the three wires that carry the message, one of them is the ground and the other two carry the exact same signal at the same time; the two signals are "in phase." Noise is likely to hit these two wires at slightly different times and not be quite the same in both wires. The noise will be "out of phase." The equipment receiving the signal lets things that are in phase pass through but will filter out things that are out of phase. Thus, much of the noise can be filtered out. For the system to work, both links of the system must be balanced. Balanced and unbalanced components can be hooked together, but you will lose the advantages of balanced audio. There are pieces of equipment that will allow you to plug in an unbalanced source and make it balanced from that point on.

Consumer equipment, then, is always high-impedance unbalanced, and professional equipment is low-impedance balanced. There is equipment that will convert high-impedance unbalanced to low-impedance balanced and low-impedance balanced to high-impedance unbalanced. This will allow you to mix consumer and professional equipment and get the best sound possible. The use of this equipment, however, is usually limited to the studio. The equipment is bulky and needs to be plugged into a power source, which makes it difficult to use it in the field.

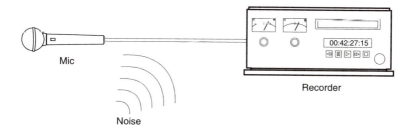

Mic

Noise

Recorder

00:42:27:15

**Unbalanced audio lets induced noise pass through.**

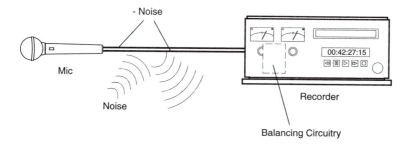

- Noise

Mic

Noise

Noise

Recorder

00:42:27:15

Balancing Circuitry

**Balanced audio filters out induced noise that is out of phase.**

# Combining Audio Components

### Line and Mic Levels

Every piece of audio equipment except for microphones produces a very strong signal. This strong signal is usually called *line-level* or a *high-level signal*. Microphones create their own electricity and as a result create very weak signals. Mic-level or low-level signals may be 40 to 60 dB weaker than line-level signals. (Refer to the section on signal-to-noise ratios for a discussion of the dB scale and how it works.) If you take the output of a microphone and plug it into an input designed for line levels, you will hear no sound out of the microphone. If you take a line-level output and plug it into a mic-level input, the line-level signal will be so strong that distorted sound will blast out of the loudspeaker. Most of us make this mistake only once.

### Analog and Digital

Even a fully digital audio system will have analog components because microphones and loudspeakers are analog components. Therefore, it is common for digital audio equipment to accept and produce analog signal. In many small and midsized facilities, it is common to have a mix of analog and digital audio equipment. Analog equipment might include microphones, loudspeakers, headphones, and even the audio mixer. (The mixer is sort of like the switcher on the video side of the system; it allows you to bring in many sound sources, choose among them, mix them together, process them, and produce a finished audio signal.) Digital equipment might include a video recorder, digital audio workstations, CD players, and so on.

### Professional and Consumer Equipment

Because a lot of consumer equipment produces very good sound and is much less expensive than professional equipment, many smaller facilities will use a mix of professional and consumer equipment. The conversion equipment can be installed in the equipment racks, and a number of companies make mixers that will accept either professional or consumer inputs.

Thus, in smaller studios it will be common to find a mix of analog, digital, professional, and consumer equipment.

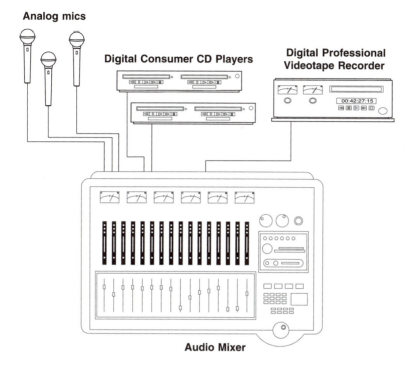

**Analog mics**

**Digital Consumer CD Players**

**Digital Professional Videotape Recorder**

00:42:27:15

**Audio Mixer**

Analog, digital, professional and consumer are often used together in the same audio system.

*The beginning, middle, and end of the audio system.*

# Microphones, Mixers, and Loudspeakers

### Microphones

To record natural sound, the first step in the system is the microphone. The *microphone* is a transducer that changes sound energy into electrical energy. All microphones will have a highly flexible diaphragm that will vibrate in sympathy with sound movements of the air. The vibrating diaphragm will create a very small electrical voltage. That small (mic-level) voltage will be passed on to the next piece of equipment in the system. So-called digital microphones will have an A to D converter attached to the diaphragm circuitry to create the digital signal. The A to D converter will require both electrical circuitry and power, thus making the microphone somewhat large and bulky. Their size makes them unsuitable in front of a video camera.

### Mixers

As mentioned earlier, the *mixer* (sometimes called the board or console) is analogous to the production switcher on the video side of the system. The mixer allows you to bring several sound sources together, choose among them, mix them together, measure their strength, and hear them. If it doesn't go through the mixer, you probably won't hear it.

Digital and analog mixers will look much the same. They will have similar looking controls to accomplish the tasks listed above. The analog mixer will deal only with analog sound, of course, but since all digital devices also produce analog sound, this is not a problem. Because digital mixers will have to deal with analog inputs such as microphones, they will have built in A to D converters to change incoming analog signals to digital. Digital mixers will also be quite a bit more expensive than analog mixers.

### Loudspeakers

The last step in the audio system is the *loudspeaker*. The loudspeaker is an analog transducer that converts electrical energy into sound energy. The loudspeaker will have a small piston wrapped in a coil of fine wire mounted inside of a magnetic field. The piston will be attached to a flexible cone. As the changing analog voltage enters the wire coil around the piston, it will create a changing electromagnetic field. That field will interact with the surrounding magnetic field, causing the piston to move back and forth. The moving piston will cause the flexible cone to move, which will cause the air to move and vibrate, thus creating sound.

**168**

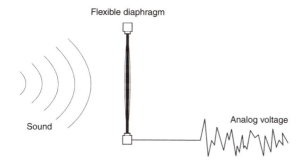

Flexible diaphragm

Sound

Analog voltage

**Microphones work by changing sound waves into analog voltage.**

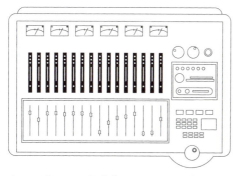

**Analog mixers allow one to bring many sound sources together.**

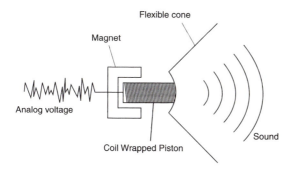

Flexible cone

Magnet

Analog voltage

Coil Wrapped Piston

Sound

**Loudspeakers change analog voltages into sound.**

*The sound must be recorded.*

# Sound Recorders for Video

For all practical purposes, analog recording is no longer used for video productions; virtually all of the video recorders and camcorders sold today are digital. For the video production person these will be the primary recording devices for both picture and sound. Most of the concepts you learned for digital video also apply to digital audio. Terms like sampling rate, quantizing, processing levels, compression, A to D converters, and D to A converters also apply to audio. There are specific differences, of course. For digital video we use high sampling rates (in the megahertz range) and relatively low processing levels (8- or 10-bit processing). For digital audio it is the opposite: low sampling rates (48,000 Hz for audio on digital videotape) and very high processing (16 bit). Audio compression is also done differently by dividing the frequency range into different bands of frequencies and compressing them separately. But the idea of removing redundancies and eliminating things you can't hear anyway to reduce bandwidth needs is similar.

The recording process is similar as well. Sound will enter the recorder from the microphone. That sound will enter an A to D converter, where it will be digitized and put down on the recording medium as a series of 0s and 1s. When the material is played back, it will go through a D to A converter and be converted back to analog sound. With the best quality machines, uncompressed audio will be recorded. In order to save bandwidth and money, lower quality machines will use compressed audio.

## DAT

Very rarely in a video production will you go out in the field and record sound without also recording the picture. If you do, you will probably use a *DAT (digital audiotape)* recorder. Like a videotape recorder, the DAT machine uses a rotating headwheel that moves in the opposite direction to the tape. While DAT recorders play and record high-quality sound, there are two major problems with them. First, the machines are somewhat delicate and have to be handled very carefully, and they are quite easy to break. Second, downloading the information to a computer for editing takes real time. That is, an hour tape takes an hour to download.

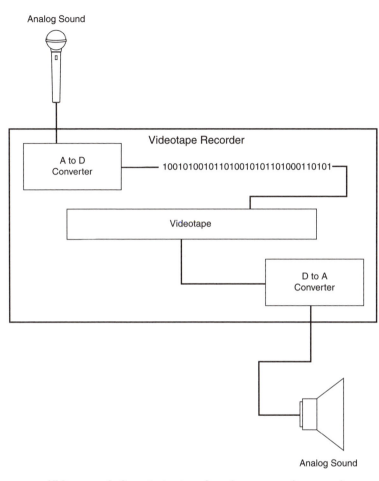

Video sound often starts at a microphone as analog sound
that is converted to digital for recording, and is reconverted to analog for
playback on a speaker.

*Sound editing is done on computers.*

# Digital Audio Workstations (DAW)

For smaller productions you will probably do whatever sound editing that is needed right on your nonlinear editor along with your video. But for high-budget sophisticated productions you will probably send your audio in the form of a computer file to a professional sound company for editing, processing, adding of sound effects and music, and so on. Most of that work will be done on a *digital audio workstation (DAW)*. Many software programs are available that will let you use your home computer as a DAW. Many of these programs are excellent, versatile, and affordable. These programs use the high-impedance unbalanced sound cards that are already in your computer. Professionals will want low-impedance balanced audio, and that will require a package that includes both software and hardware. Some of these packages can cost $50,000 or more! Luckily, many of the companies that make the professional packages also make low-cost consumer software that shares the same look and many features of their professional packages.

Most of these packages allow for complex editing, sound effects and processing, and multiple tracks so that you can deal with each sound component separately. Most will have time codes so that the sound can be synchronized with video. To work best, these systems need very fast computers with lots of memory and disc space. These features allow even the smallest companies to do a level of audio work that only the biggest studios could afford a few years ago.

One of the easiest ways to ruin an otherwise good video production is by having poor sound. Bad sound will destroy all of the good parts of your production. With the tools available today, there is no reason to tolerate poor sound.

Digital audio workstations start with high-powered home computers.

Consumer and professional DAWs will add sophisticated software.

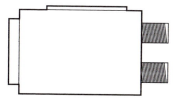

Professional DAW packages will also have specialized hardware to go with the software.

# Further Reading

ALTEN, STANLEY:
*Audio in media*, 6th ed. Belmont, CA: Wadsworth, 2001.

ANDERSON, GARY H.:
*Video Editing and Post-production: A Professional Guide*, 4th ed. Boston: Focal Press, 1998.

BROWNE, STEVEN E:
*Nonlinear Editing Basics: Electronic Film and Video Editing*. Boston: Focal Press, 1998.
*Video Editing: A Postproduction Primer*, 3rd ed. Boston: Focal Press, 1997.

KALLENBERGER, RICHARD H., and CVJETNICANIN, GEORGE D.:
*Film into Video: A Guide to Merging the Technologies*, 2nd ed. Boston: Focal Press, 2000.

MILLERSON, GERALD:
*Effective TV Production*, 3rd ed. Boston and London: Focal Press, 1994.
*Lighting for Television and Film*, 3rd ed. Boston and London: Focal Press, 1999.
*Television Production*, 13th ed. Boston and London: Focal Press, 1999.

OHANIAN, THOMAS A.:
*Digital Nonlinear Editing: Editing Film and Video on the Desktop*, 2nd ed. Boston: Focal Press, 1998.

PAULSEN, KARL:
*Video and Media Servers: Technology and Applications*. Boston: Focal Press, 1998.

RUMSEY, FRANCIS, and WATKINSON, JOHN:
*The Digital Interface Handbook*, 3rd ed. Boston and London: Focal Press, 2003.

WATKINSON, JOHN:
*The Art of Digital Audio*, 3rd ed. Boston and London: Focal Press, 2000.

WHITAKER JERRY:
*DTV: The Revolution in Digital Video*, New York: McGraw-Hill, 1999.

WURTZEL, ALAN, and ROSENBAUM, JOHN:
*Television Production*, 4th ed. New York: McGraw-Hill, 1995.

ZETTL, HERBERT:
*Television Production Handbook*, 8th ed. Belmont, CA: Wadsworth, 2002.

# Glossary

**Additive colors**   The color system that mixes colored light to create all the various colors of the color spectrum.

**Algorithms**   Complex mathematical formulas that define digital compression.

**Alternating current**   An electrical circuit through which the flow of electrons reverses itself from negative to positive, from positive to negative, and back again at a regular rate.

**Amperes (amps)**   The unit of measurement for current.

**Analog video signal**   The varying voltages that make up the video information of a television signal.

**Assemble edits**   Edits that lay down all aspects of the signal — audio, video, and control track — all at the same time.

**A to D converter**   The circuitry that converts analog signal information into digital information.

**Audio board**   See **Audio mixer**.

**Audio console**   See **Audio mixer**.

**Audio-follows-video switcher**   A switcher that changes both audio and video sources with the push of one button.

**Audio mixer**   An audio device that allows you to bring several sound sources together, choose among them, mix them together, measure their strength, and hear them.


**Back porch**   The portion of the waveform scan that represents the horizontal blanking just before the start of a new line of video.

**Balanced audio**   A technology used with professional sound equipment designed to reduce the amount of induced electromagnetic noise in the audio system.

**Bandwidth**   The amount of space available over the airwaves or through a cable for carrying information. A signal with more information requires more bandwidth to carry it.

**Bit**   The smallest increment of computer memory represented by a 0 or a 1.

**Black burst**   A signal from the sync generator that includes all normal blanking and sync information along with black video.

**Blanking**   That time when the electron guns in the system are turned down to a low voltage so that they can return to the beginning of a new line or field.

**Blanking pulses**   Signals from the sync generator that tell the camera's electron gun to go into blanking.

**Bus**   A row of buttons on a switcher that allows a person to change between various video sources that are available in the system.

**Byte**   The smallest piece of computer memory that can be used as a distinct piece of information; made up of a group of bits.

**Camera**   A device that changes light images into a usable electronic signal.

**Capstan servo**   See **Vertical lock**.

**CCD (charge-coupled device)**   A solid-state device used instead of a pickup tube for changing light images into an electronic video signal.

**Character generator (CG)**   A machine that creates words and titles for the TV screen.

**Chroma**   The color information in a TV signal.

**Chroma key**   A special effect in which a chosen color is replaced with video from another source.

**Chroma key tracking**   A digital effect that compresses the signal from a video source into the available chroma key window.

**CODEC**   Stands for code/decode and defines all of the technical parameters of a digital format.

**Color burst** or **3.58**   The color reference inserted in every video line that determines how color information is to be interpreted.

**Color difference component video**   A component video system that saves bandwidth by using a luminance channel (Y), which comes primarily from the green channel, and two color channels with the luminance removed (R-Y and B-Y).

**Color subcarrier**   See **Color burst**.

**Color sync**   See **Color burst**.

**Complementary colors**   The colors cyan, magenta, and yellow that are created by mixing parts of the primary colors (red, green, and blue).

**Component switcher**   A video switcher that deals with the individual color components (red, green, and blue) of the picture instead of the encoded composite video signal.

**Component video**   A video signal made up of the individual component parts as opposed to an encoded composite signal.

**Composite video**   The video signal made up of both the video and sync information.

**Compressions**   Digital effects in which the size and/or aspect of the picture is changed on the TV screen.

**Compression, Spatial**   Video compression that takes place within an individual video frame that contributes to overall bandwidth reduction.

**178**

**Compression, Temporal**   Video compression that takes place between successive video frames which helps reduce overall bandwidth needs.

**Compression, Video**   Removal of redundant information and encoding of video in such a way that it can be transmitted and stored using less bandwidth than uncompressed video.

**Control track**   A track on the videotape used to help stabilize tape playback speed.

**Control track counter editing controller**   A device that controls videotape editing by counting the control track pulses on the tapes.

**CRT (cathode ray tube)**   Television picture tube.

**Current**   The volume of electrons passing a given point at a given time, measured in amps.

**DA (distribution amplifier)**   A piece of equipment that produces multiple outputs identical to its input signal.

**DAT (digital audiotape)**   Equipment that uses a small audiocassette and a recording head mounted on a spinning drum that moves in the opposite direction to the tape.

**Dedicated equipment**   Video equipment designed for a specific purpose, such as switchers, edit controllers, and character generators.

**Deflection yoke**   Electromagnetic coils around a CRT used to steer the CRT's electron beam as it sprays the picture across the screen.

**Desktop video**   The concept of private individuals being able to do low-cost, high-quality video production using production equipment based on the personal computer.

**Digital audio workstation (DAW)**   A computer system with specialized software and possibly hardware that allows the computer to record, edit, and process multiple audio tracks into a finished sound product.

**Digital encoding ratios**   A ratio that indicates the relationship between the amount of luminance (Y), and chrominance (B-Y and R-Y). Information is contained in a digital signal, for example, 4:2:2 or 4:1:1.

**Digital video**   A video signal that is made up of a series of assigned numbers rather than analog voltages.

**Direct current**   An electrical circuit through which the flow of electrons moves in only one direction.

**Disc-based recorders**   Video recorders that use either magnetic discs like computer hard drives or optical discs like DVDs in place of videotape for recording.

**Drive pulses**   Signals from the sync generator that control the scanning of the electron beams.

**D to A converter**   Circuitry that converts digital information into analog information.

**Drop frame**   When set in the drop frame mode SMPTE time code will consistently skip a number in the sequence. Since time code normally counts 30 frames a second when video really only has 29.97 frames a second, this is necessary so that the time code can be consistent with the real time on a clock.

**Dubbing**   The process of copying the electronic signal from one tape to another.

**Dynamic tracking head**   A videotape head that automatically aligns itself with the center of the video track on the tape for slow motion or freeze frames.

**EDL** or **edit decision list**   Editing script that includes SMPTE time code start and stop points, running time, and transition types. It is usually put together during the off-line editing process.

**Electronic palette**   A rectangular surface that represents the "paper" in a computer graphics system.

**Encoding**   The process of combining the chroma and luminance information into a single signal.

**Fields**   The complete set of odd- or even-numbered lines that, when interlaced, make up one video frame.

**5.1 sound**   A surround sound system that has been accepted as part of the HDTV standard for the United States.

**Flow diagrams**   A diagram that uses geometric shapes and lines in place of equipment and wires to illustrate the interconnection of equipment.

**Fonts**   The style of a particular typeface that is used on a character generator.

**Frame**   In the U.S. system, two interlaced fields of 262.5 lines each, which, when combined, make a complete picture of 525 lines. There are 30 frames per second in the NTSC (American) system.

**Frame lock**   A method of stabilizing videotape playback that tries to match an even field of the playback signal to an even field coming from the sync generator, and an odd field of the playback signal to an odd field coming from the sync generator.

**Frame store synchronizer (frame synchronizer)**   A device used to lock up nonsynchronous video signals to the main system.

**Front porch**   The portion of the waveform scan that represents the horizontal blanking at the end of a line of video.

**180**

**Giga (G)**   The abbreviation for billions (1,000,000,000). For example, 6 GHz would equal 6,000,000,000 Hz.

**Gyroscopic time base error**   Time base error that is created when a videotape recorder is moved perpendicular to the plane of the head drum's rotation.

**HDTV**   High-definition TV.

**Head**   The small electromagnetic device that lays down or picks up the information on a piece of recording tape.

**Headwheel**   The rotating disc on which the video heads are mounted.

**Helical**   A method of video recording that lays down video information at a slant to the tape's direction of travel; also known as slant track recording.

**Hertz (Hz)**   A measurement of frequency equal to one cycle per second.

**Horizontal blanking**   The period extending from the time the electron guns are turned down to a low voltage at the end of a line until they are turned back up at the beginning of a new line.

**Horizontal lock**   A method of stabilizing videotape playback that tries to match a horizontal sync pulse of the playback signal to each horizontal sync pulse coming from the sync generator.

**Horizontal sync**   The signal from the sync generator that causes the electron gun to return to the other side of the screen for a new line.

**Impedance**   A measurement of the properties that tell whether two or more circuits will interact well — measured in ohms.

**Induction**   The process in which a circuit with a stronger magnetic field forces some of its signal into a circuit with a weaker magnetic field.

**Insert edits**   Edits that use control tracks that have already been laid down on the tape.

**Interlace scanning**   The process of taking a field of odd-numbered lines (1, 3, 5, 7, . . .) and combining it with a field of even-numbered lines (2, 4, 6, 8, . . .) to make a complete video frame (525).

**Interpolation**   The mathematical process of creating new video information (pixels) from surrounding information.

**Keys**   A special effect in which the signal from one video source "cuts" a hole into another video source.

**Kilo (K)**   The abbreviation for thousand (5 K = 5000).

**LCD (liquid crystal display)**   A flat-screen monitor where liquid crystals control light to create a picture.

**Linear editing**   The traditional method of videotape editing in which one scene is laid down after another on tape. If any changes are needed after the edits have been made, the rest of the tape will have to be reedited.

**Linear keys**   Keys in which the key hole is not cut entirely through the background video, allowing that video to be seen through the overlying key.

**Loudspeaker**   An audio transducer that changes analog voltages into sound.

**Luminance**   The black and white portion of the video signal.

**Luminance keys**   Keys in which the hole being cut is determined by the brightness of the video source.

**Manual editing**   Editing that is performed completely by a person without using an electronic editing controller.

**Matte key**   A luminance key whereby the "hole" created by the key is filled with artificially created color from the switcher.

**Mega (M)**   The abbreviation for million (3 M= 3,000,000).

**Micro (μ)**   The abbreviation for millionth (5 μ = 5/1,000,000).

**Microphone**   An audio transducer that changes sound into analog voltages.

**Milli (m)**   The abbreviation for thousandth (200 m = 200/1000).

**Mismatch**   Refers to impedance in which two pieces of equipment will not work well together.

**Monitor**   A TV set designed to display a straight video signal as opposed to a set designed to receive programs off the air.

**Mono or monaural sound**   Sound where the entire sonic message is recorded on one channel and played through one speaker.

**MPEG 2 (Moving Picture Experts Group 2)**   The most commonly used professional video compression standard.

**Nano (n)**   The abbreviation for billionth (5 n = 5/1,000,000,000).

**Noise**   Unwanted electromagnetic static inherent in all electronic circuits.

**Noncomposite video**   Video information without sync information.

**Nonlinear editing**   A method in which video information is recorded into a digital memory where it can be called up a piece at a time in any order desired. Changes can be made in the edited program without reediting the entire show.

**Nonsynchronous**   A signal that is completely out of sync with the main system.

**NTSC**   The system of color television used in the United States and other parts of the world. The system uses 525 scanning lines and 60 fields

**182**

with 30 frames per second. (The field and frame rates have been rounded off.) Tho namo comes from the National Television Systems Committee, which was a group of industry experts who developed and proposed the system to the Federal Communications Commission in the early 1950s.

**Off-line editing**   The process of developing an editing script made up of SMPTE code numbers and a work print on small-format helical equipment.
**Ohm ($\Omega$)**   The unit of measurement for both resistance and impedance.
**On-air switcher**   The switcher used to determine what goes to the transmitter; usually an audio-follows-video switcher.
**On-line editing**   The process of editing the final, finished tape on large-format tape machines.
**Open architecture**   The concept of using computers with highly specialized programs to replace traditional dedicated equipment. Hence, a computer could be a time base corrector, edit controller, video switcher, digital effects unit, and character generator, all in one.
**Out of phase**   A condition that occurs when cameras show different colors during a transition because their color bursts are not matched.
**Oxides**   The coating on tape that allows signals to be recorded magnetically.

**Pages**   In a character generator or computer graphics system, one full screen of information that can be displayed at a time.
**PAL (Phase Alternate Lines)**   A color television system that was designed in Germany to overcome some of the problems of NTSC; it uses 625 scanning lines with 50 fields and 25 frames per second. This system is used in Western Europe and many other parts of the world.
**PAL-M**   A color television system that is the same as PAL except that it is designed for countries that use a 60-Hz frequency for their AC power supply and therefore has 60 fields and 30 frames per second.
**Patch panel**   A device that allows flexible routing of signals from one place to another.
**Pedestal**   The black portions or areas of the TV picture.
**Pixel**   Picture element.
**Plasma display screen**   A video display device that uses electrically charged gases (plasma) to activate color pixels.
**Primary colors**   In television, the colors red, green, and blue.
**Proc amp**   Video processing amplifier, a piece of equipment that strips the distorted sync from a videotape playback signal and replaces it with clean sync. Most proc amps also allow the control of some of the video parameters, such as hue, video brightness, and pedestal (black) levels.

**Progressive scanning**   This is when a CRT electron gun scans the picture from top to bottom in numerical order; lines 1, 2, 3, 4, 5, . . .

**Quantizing**   The process of converting a sample of video information into a number.

**Resistance**   A measurement in ohms indicating the constraint to the flow of electricity.

**Routing switcher**   A switcher used to route signals from one place to another.

**Sampling**   The process of "grabbing" a piece of analog video information so that it can be quantized, or converted into numbers, for either processing or storage in memory.

**SDTV (standard definition digital television)**   The digital equal to the analog color standard that has been in use for decades; what you get with the mini-dish satellite or digital cable systems.

**Self-fill key**   A luminance key in which the hole cut is filled by the video that cut the hole.

**Signal-to-noise ratio**   A comparison of the strength of the signal coming out of a piece of equipment to the internal noise created by that equipment.

**SMPTE**   Society of Motion Picture and Television Engineers. This is the professional organization of electrical engineers that focuses on motion picture and broadcast technology.

**SMPTE time code**   A digital code laid down on tape that gives each frame of video a unique and unchanging address (03:38:52:04 would equal 3 hours, 38 minutes, 52 seconds, and 4 frames).

**Software**   Computer programming that tells the computer how to process information.

**Stereo** or **stereophonic sound**   Sound that is recorded on multiple channels and played through multiple speakers to give the sense that sound is coming from different locations.

**Stylus**   An electronic device that acts as the pen, pencil, brush, and the like, in a computer graphics system.

**Surround sound**   A type of stereo using speakers all around a room to give the sense that sound is coming from anywhere in the room.

**Switcher**   A device that allows a person to make a transition between video sources.

**Sync**   A signal from the sync generator that causes the electron guns to return to the beginning of a new video line or field.

**Sync generator**   A device that provides various sync signals (drive pulses, blanking pulses, and sync pulses) to keep all of the equipment in a video system working together.

**Tape transport system**   The mechanical system that pulls tape through a machine at an even speed.

**Target**   The photosensitive coating of a pickup tube.

**TBC (time base corrector)**   A device for correcting time base error in videotape playback.

**Time base error**   The instability of a videotape playback signal created by the machine's inability to play back at exactly the same speed at which the tape was recorded.

**Transparent key**   See **Linear keys**.

**Unbalanced audio**   Audio that does not have the aspects of balanced audio (see **Balanced audio**); used on consumer audio equipment.

**Vectorscope**   A piece of equipment that shows a graphic display of the color portion of the video signal.

**Vertical blanking**   The period when the electron beam is turned down at the end of a video field until it is turned back up at the start of a new field.

**Vertical interval**   The period when the electron beam is in vertical blanking.

**Vertical interval switcher**   A switcher that delays cuts between video sources until the entire system is in vertical blanking.

**Vertical lock**   A method of stabilizing videotape playback that tries to match the control track pulses of the playback signal to vertical sync pulses coming from the sync generator; also called capstan servo.

**Vertical sync**   The signal from the sync generator that tells the electron beams to return to the top of the screen for the start of a new video field.

**Video compression**   A technology that allows digital video information to be compressed into a smaller space, thereby requiring less bandwidth or memory space for transmission or storage.

**Video servers**   Computer-like hard drives specially designed to record and play back multiple channels of video information.

**Volt**   The measurement for the pressure of electricity.

**Voltage**   The pressure of electricity, measured in volts.

**VTR (videotape recorder)**   A machine that records sound and pictures onto magnetic tape.

**Watt**  A measurement of electrical power.

**Waveform monitor**  A piece of equipment that shows a graphic display of the black and white portion of the video signal.

**Window of correction**  The amount of time base error a time base corrector will correct, measured in video lines.

**Y/C**  Y equals the luminance portion, and C equals the chrominance portion of the video signal. A Y/C piece of equipment or system will keep the components separate as much as possible.

# Index